Palm
Reading

The marks on your hand may be interpreted in a variety of ways. Experienced palm readers may give different readings of the same hand. Should you be interested in finding out more, please consult a reputable palm reader.

HarperCollins Publishers
77-85 Fulham Palace Road
Hammersmith
London W6 8JB

www.collins.co.uk

A Diagram book first created by Diagram Visual Information Limited of 195 Kentish Town Road, London NW5 2JU

Editors: Bridget Giles, Jane Johnson
Photography: PS5 Limited

First published 2000

This edition published 2005

Reprint 10 9 8 7

ISBN-13 978-0-00-718880-2
ISBN-10 0-00-718880-3

Printed in China by Leo Paper

Foreword

Collins Gem Palm Reading reveals the ancient art of palmistry. With easy-to-follow diagrams accompanying clear and concise text, this books lays bare the complexities of hand reading so that even a beginner will soon be able to uncover the hidden truths of the hand. Yet there is enough detail included in the coverage to make the book a must on any palmist's shelves, beginner or otherwise.

If the outward forms are the visible aspects of the interior patterns, it is possible from the study of certain external characteristics to go back to the psychic causes to which they are related.

Plato, Greek philosopher (c. 428–c. 348 BC)

God has placed signs in the hands of all the sons of men, that all the sons of men may know his work.

The Bible

...modern biology...does not exclude the possibility that hands, whose shape and function are so intimately connected with the psyche, might provide revealing, and therefore interpretable, expression of...the human character...

Carl Jung, Swiss psychiatrist (1875–1961)

4

Contents

Introduction

Palmistry is a misleading name, for a great deal more than the palm of the hand is considered in this type of prediction. The experts prefer more resonantly impressive terms like 'cheirognomy', 'cheirology' or even 'cheiromancy', from the Greek word *cheir,* meaning 'hand'. But whatever you choose to call it, it remains a process rooted in the belief that you literally hold your future in your hands.

HISTORY

People have always been fascinated by the markings on their hands – palm prints have even been discovered in Stone Age cave paintings. Although no physical evidence exists to support their theories, some practitioners have claimed that the origins of palmistry lie far back with the ancient Egyptians, Chaldeans, Sumerians or Babylonians. It seems likely that palmistry began in the east and spread to the west, perhaps carried by the Romany peoples.

A page from Saunders' *Palmistry: The Secrets thereof Disclosed*

The earliest verifiable references to the art seem to be in Indian literature of the Vedic period (c. 2000 BC) in the east, and in the works of Aristotle (384–322 BC) in the west – but both these bear witness to a rich history of oral tradition on the subject.

Lines are not written in to the human hand without reason; they emanate from heavenly influences and man's own individuality

Aristotle

Palmistry has had a chequered history: in the 17th century it was taught at the universities of Leipzig and Halle in Germany, while at the same time it was being outlawed in England as a form of witchcraft.

WHY READ HANDS?

There are thousands of nerve endings in your hands which are in direct contact with your brain, and so there is a constant two-way traffic of impulses along the nerves. Because of this traffic, the lines and marks on your hands are supposed to show a reflection of your personality, to mirror your physical and emotional condition. Palmists have always known this intuitively: today's scientists are finding evidence to support the theory, and some geneticists and psychiatrists already use hand analysis to assist them in the diagnosis of a variety of physical and mental illnesses.

MAP OF THE HAND

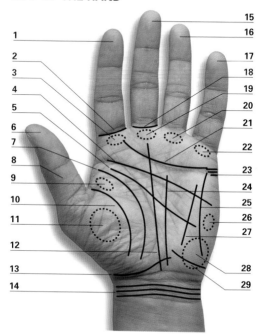

1 Finger of Jupiter	16 Finger of Apollo
2 Solomon's ring	17 Finger of Mercury
3 Mount of Jupiter	18 Ring of Saturn
4 Heartline	19 Mount of Saturn
5 Headline	20 Mount of Apollo
6 Phalange of will	21 Girdle of Venus
7 Lifeline	22 Mount of Mercury
8 Phalange of logic	23 Line of marriage
9 Lower mount of Mars	24 Line of the sun
10 Line of Mars	25 Line of intuition
11 Mount of Venus	26 Upper mount of Mars
12 Line of Fate	27 Hepatica
13 Via Lasciva	28 Mount of the moon
14 Rascettes	29 Child lines
15 Finger of Saturn	

1. Getting Started

GIVING A READING

When you are preparing to read someone's hands, make
sure you have somewhere comfortable for you both to sit.
Arrange both the chairs so that you are not awkwardly
facing each other but so that you are almost side by side.
You should be able to comfortably hold the person's hand
in yours without having to analyze it upside down.

**Aerial view of a suitable seating
plan for giving a reading**

overhead
light source

chairs

As a novice palmist, you may find that you need to take
notes or keep a list handy of what to look at on the hand.
You can use the following list as a reminder of what needs
to considered for a complete reading:

- hand shape
- development of the palmar quadrants
- skin texture and hairiness
- hand position

- fingers: shape, flexibility, set, joints, fingertips, fingernails and fingerprints
- if you have time, an individual assessment of each finger can be very revealing
- the thumb: shape, flexibility, angle, phalanges
- mounts
- lines on the hand
- marks on the mounts, lines and phalanges

The cardinal rule in palmistry, as in all the major forms of character analysis, is that an overall view is essential. You cannot hope to achieve any certain picture of your subject's character and potential from only the shape of the hand, or from any other isolated detail. You must wait until all the clues have been gathered and see then how one factor balances or compensates for another, how different elements are reinforced, others cancelled out and so on.

This paramount rule partly explains why good palmists rarely make sweeping, unequivocal statements along the lines of 'you will be rich this time next year' or 'you have only six months to live'. There are too many factors in a subject as broad and complex as palmistry. They cannot be interpreted simply, in the way of the omens of folk belief, or the flat assertions of newspaper horoscopes. What you achieve, when all the details are collated, is a probable pattern, a set of tendencies, with very little in it of fixed, unavoidable fate. Every reading, like every human being, is a mixture of good and bad.

Therefore, always remember when giving a reading that you should mix positive news with negative news, and be wary of being the voice of doom unless you are more than 100% certain of your analysis. Think first what will the person do with the information you are giving them? If it will just serve to depress and demotivate them, then perhaps you need to reconsider the need to impart every truth you see (or think you see) in the hand.

FURTHER POINTS TO REMEMBER

First, be careful. Real hands seldom show marks as clearly as do the illustrations in this book, and you will need to have studied a great many hands before you can be completely confident in your recognition of detail. Second, be open-minded. Don't leap to conclusions about the nature of a hand, for there is then the temptation to ignore other details, or subconsciously to twist their meaning, when they do not conform to your too-hasty interpretation. Let your reading build slowly, and accept all the contradictions, divergences and inconsistencies.

Third, remember to correlate all the details into a complete, balanced picture before delivering your interpretation. Most people get along through life fairly well, with plenty of ups and downs, good times and bad, in general balancing each other out. Try to find a similar kind of balance in your readings. And finally, consider the chirognomists' assertion that destiny as revealed in the hand is not fixed and predetermined. The lines and marks can change, it is said, over a period of time, as obviously can the fleshiness of the fingers and mounts. And so good or ill omens may in fact come and go.

MAKING A PRINT

There is much to be said for reading a hand from a print, rather than the hand itself. You will be in no danger of being affected by the subject's possible reactions to your comments as you build up the reading. And if you keep the print safely, some years later you can determine for yourself whether the hands have changed in any of the details – and if so what those changes may indicate.

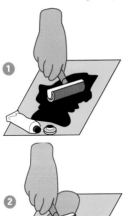

1 The easiest way to produce a good print is with a small roller. Squeeze out some ink (water-based for easy removal) onto a smooth surface, and pass the roller through it several times.

2 Then use the roller to transfer a thin film of ink as evenly as possible to all the surfaces of the palm, fingers and thumb.

3 Make the print by pressing the subject's hand carefully but firmly on to a sheet of paper, making sure that you get a good impression of the centre of the palm as well as the fingers and thumb – a rubber pad under the paper will be helpful.

4 Lift the hand away carefully, making sure that you do not blur the print. Make a note of the date and the name of the print's owner on the back of the paper after it has dried.

RIGHT AND LEFT HANDS

Which hand you read is very important. Your left hand is said to indicate the potentialities that you were born with, and your right hand to reveal your individual nature as it is now, and what its future may be – unless you are left-handed, when the reverse applies. The differences can be usefully revealing of the directions the subject has taken through life, and of the effect of the years on the subject.

If you can, find out which hand is the person's dominant one: that is, the one they write with or use the most. Generally, the right hand is the dominant one, and it is the dominant hand that reveals most about a person's present life and character; the other hand is more revealing of the past. Comparison of the two hands can reveal much about how someone has evolved and developed as they mature.

DOMINANT AND PASSIVE HAND ASSOCIATIONS

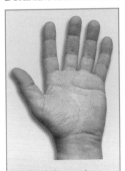

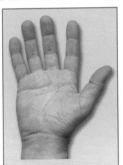

Passive left reveals:
- past
- childhood
- parental influence
- intuitive, instinctive thinking
- potential abilities
- hereditary factors

Dominant right reveals:
- present
- adulthood
- evolving self-identity
- rational, conscious thought
- achievements
- how talents are put to use

2. The Whole Hand

REGIONS OF THE HAND

Over the centuries that palmistry developed, different regions of the hand came to be seen to represent particular aspects of the world, both seen and unseen, and different aspects of the personality. There are two main ways to section the hand. It can be divided into thirds: 'the three worlds', or it can be divided into quarters: the palmar quadrants. The division of a hand into the three worlds brings a metaphysical slant to character analysis while each of the palmar quadrants is regarded as being related to a particular facet of the personality.

THE THREE WORLDS

Under this system, the first world is represented by the fingers, the second by the top half of the palm and the third by the base of the palm. It is important to note which is the physically dominant section of the hand: which region is largest in proportion to the others? The relative size of the region is linked to the importance of that realm to the person. Each region has a variety of names.

FIRST WORLD

The first word is also referred to as the mental, ideal or intellectual world. It is linked to a person's spiritual nature. The larger this realm (that is, the longer the fingers), the more spiritual the individual. To understand more about this region of the hand, read the chapter on fingers.

SECOND WORLD

The second world is also called the material, or apparently paradoxically, the celestial world. These two names reveal the regions links to a person's dealings with the world, both seen and unseen. It tells us about their position in life and their business acumen, in particular, but also about their emotional lives. A large material world shows that a person can balance practical and emotional aspects of their lives. To understand more about this region of the hand, read the sections on lines, the thumb and the mounts of Jupiter, Saturn, Apollo and Mercury.

First world

Second world

Third world

THIRD WORLD

The third world is also called the hidden, baser or elemental world. It is linked to a person's subconscious and base instincts. This region contains the mount of Moon, which is the seat of the imagination. To understand more about the third world, read the sections on the palmar quadrants and the mounts of Venus, the Moon and Mars.

PALMAR QUADRANTS

Divide the palm into fourths (quadrants) by drawing an imaginary line from the centre of the base of the middle finger to the centre of the base of the palm, dividing the palm into two. Another line runs across the middle of the palm, creating the quadrants. Each quadrant represents one of the four elements: Earth, Fire, Air and Water.

ASSESSING DOMINANCE

As with the three worlds, it is important to see which quadrant (or half; see below) dominates the hand to understand what preoccupies and defines a particular person. Sometimes it is possible to see which is the dominant quadrant just by visually ranking them according to size. It is not always so obvious however. On a print, look for darker regions since these indicate more developed regions. On an actual hand, note the relative size of mounts to see which ones are largest, and check the distribution of lines between quadrants. Dominant quadrants are identifiable for having the greater proportion of the hand's lines.

HALVES

The right and left halves, and the upper and lower halves, also have distinct associations. The thumb side of the palm (earth and fire quadrants) is linked with the visible and manifest aspects of a person's outer appearance. The little finger side of the palm (Air and Water quadrants) is linked with the hidden, non-manifest aspects of a person's inner life, including their dreams and ideals. The solar region is

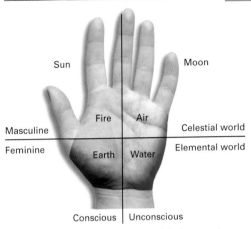

associated with conscious thought, and the lunar region with subconscious thought.

The upper half of the palm (Fire and Air quadrants) is basically the same region that is called the second, or celestial, world. The lower half of the palm (Earth and Water quadrants) is the third, or elemental, world. The celestial half is associated with supposedly masculine traits such as activity, motivation and aspiration. The elemental half is concerned with supposedly feminine traits such as stability, passivity and materialism. The upper half reflects mental concerns, the lower physical.

▪ FIRE QUADRANT

The Fire quadrant can be described as the
outer active area. It relates to social
attitudes and relationships with the
outside world and to how a person
expresses their energy. Energy can be
expressed creatively or stressfully. It is
a quadrant of mental, rational
thought and can reveal a person's
ambition, logic and achievements. A
person who has a dominant fire quadrant
is ambitious and suited for a career in
industry, engineering, sport or the armed forces. If the Fire
quadrant is underdeveloped, a lack of confidence is
revealed.

▪ AIR QUADRANT

The Air quadrant can be described as the
inner active area. It relates to a person's
close relationships and sexuality, since
it is concerned in particular with
matters of communication. The air
quadrant reveals truths about a
person's thoughts, ideas and how they
express themselves. While this region
is still concerned with mental thoughts,
it is located within the instinctive,
subconscious realm. When this region
dominates the hand, the person will be driven to express
themselves creatively. Ideal careers involve music, art,
entertainment, education, writing, science, media and

computing. Physiologically, the air quadrant is connected with the nervous and respiratory systems.

■ EARTH QUADRANT

The Earth quadrant can also be described as the outer passive area. It relates to energy and creative potential, but the creativity is channelled into practical ends, often concerned with physical gratification, though, rather than mental rewards. A person's skeletal and digestive systems are connected to their earth quadrant. This region is not all about base instincts, though. Someone with a well-developed earth quadrant will quite probably be in tune with nature, and often themselves. Stability, material comforts and security are important.

■ WATER QUADRANT

The Water quadrant can be called the inner passive area. It relates to the subconscious. This is a physical but intuitive zone, concerned with innate and learned aspects of a person's instinctive behaviour. If this area is dominant, that person is sensitive and spiritual. If it is underdeveloped, that person is probably so down-to-earth they have lost touch with their inner selves.

HAND SHAPE: CHEIROTYPES

A person's cheirotype is decided by the shape of the hand and the length and shape of the fingers. It is therefore revealed by cheirognomy: the study of the hand's physique, as it were. A person's cheirotype can be as revealing as the lines on the palm of the hand, but should ideally be read in conjunction with other factors revealed by a complete hand reading.

There are a variety of classification systems used to establish a person's cheirotype. Traditionally, fortune tellers asserted that there were seven basic types of hand shape. And these seven revealed some equally traditional attitudes to society and its hierarchy – for at one end was the delicate, languid hand of the aristocrat, and at the other was the peasant's coarsened and work-hardened fist. But even so, there may be useful clues to be gained in your own readings from this old classification, and the seven types deserve to be briefly noted.

These days, however, palmists are more ready to admit that these seven rigid classifications are somewhat unrealistic. So modern palmists have refined their classification of cheirotypes into only four or five basic types, which do tend more or less to occur in reality. They also keep a traditional flavour by relating them to the four elements of the ancient world – earth, fire, water and air – which are linked in turn with corresponding character traits.

TRADITIONAL HAND CLASSIFICATIONS

All hand classification systems can be said to divide hands into two basic types: square or conical. All other hand types are considered to be variations on these two main types. The palms of square hands are as broad as they are long, while the palms of conical hands are longer than they are wide and are often tapering from base to finger tip.

The seven traditional cheirotypes have three square hand types – the elemental, the square and the philosophical hand – and two conical types: the artistic and the psychic. The two remaining types – the spatulate and the mixed hand – can be either square or conical in their basic palm shape.

1 Elemental, or basic, hand A thick, broad, short-fingered hand. Fingertips are often square. Associated with physically strong, hard-working people. The possessor was thought to be a slow-thinker, perhaps with a crude, physical nature.

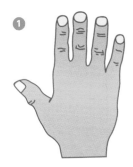

2 Square, or useful, hand
A square palm, with broad and blunt fingers. These hands were thought to indicate a conventional, unintellectual person. The owners are above all practical and hard-working, able to turn their hands to most tasks in a methodical manner. Responsible and reliable, they are blessed with integrity and stubbornness as well as patience.

3 Spatulate A spade-shaped and straight-fingered hand. Palm is generally wider at base than top but can be either square or conical (i.e. rectangular) in overall shape. The key factor is the presence of fingertips that are broad at the top. Owners of such hands are said to be independent, original, inventive figures, with a flair for science and engineering.

4 Philosophical hand

Broad-palmed, angular shape, with heavy joints on the fingers. Fingertips are saucerlike, fingers are long. These hands indicate a logical, cautious nature, thoughtful and introverted, analytic rather than fanciful. The possessors of this chirotype are often loners not given to social niceties.

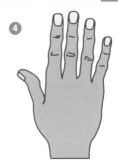

5 Artistic, or conic, hand

A long and flexible hand with tapering fingers. Palm shape is conical and fingertips rounded. As the name suggests, this chirotype indicates artistic and creative people. Owners of artistic hands have sensitive, creative natures, and are more impulsive and instinctive than methodical. These people are also romantics who can be flighty, and they lack patience or staying power.

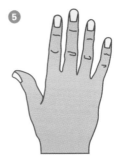

6 Idealistic, or psychic, hand An even longer and more delicate and graceful hand than the artistic hand. Fingertips are pointed rather than rounded and fingers are very long. Psychic hands reveal a nature far removed from harsh reality. The owners are dreamers, mystics, and aesthetes, ill-suited to practical tasks. They lack reason and commonsense but can be highly intuitive if not actually psychic.

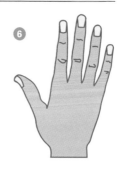

7 Mixed hand A necessary, if vague, category, since almost no-one fits precisely into just one of the foregoing six pigeonholes. Most people's hands combine two or more of the types mentioned, as do most people's natures.

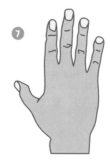

MODERN HAND CLASSIFICATIONS

Modern hand classification systems are more methodical in their approach and take greater account of the infinite variety of hand and finger shapes found in reality. The first stage in assessing the shape of a hand is to determine the relative proportions of the palm and fingers. Take the measurements indicated by X, Y and Z below:

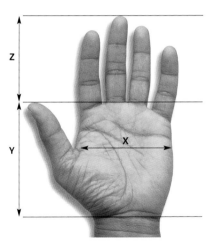

X = palm width   **Y** = palm length   **Z** = finger length

These measurements can be used to accurately calculate
the relative proportions of palm width to palm length
(factor P) and the relative proportions of finger length to
palm length (factor F). Use the equations below to
calculate factor P and factor F:

Calculating factor P

$$P = \frac{X}{X + Y} \times 100$$

Calculating factor F

$$F = \frac{Z}{Z + X} \times 100$$

FINGERTIP SHAPE

There are five basic fingertip shapes that also need to be
taken into account when assessing someone's cheirotype:

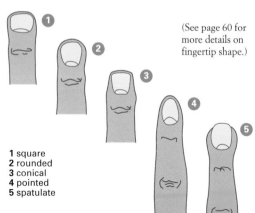

(See page 60 for
more details on
fingertip shape.)

1 square
2 rounded
3 conical
4 pointed
5 spatulate

Based on this information, use the this chart to work out your modern cheirotype:

Cheirotype	P factor	F factor	Fingertip shape
Earth	more than 46	less than 48	square or spatulate fingertips
Fire	46 or 45	49 or 50	rounded, spatulate, or square fingertips
Water	less than 43	more than 53	pointed or rounded fingertips
Air	44 or 45	51 or 52	conical, spatulate, or rounded fingertips

You may well find that your cheirotype falls into more than one category. In such situations read the analysis of both cheirotypes. A complete hand reading should indicate which is the more dominant cheirotype if it is not immediately obvious from the balance of the above factors.

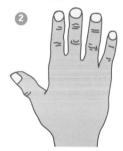

Earth hand (practical)

A square palm with short fingers (**1**). An honest, hard-working, feet-on-the-ground person. In extreme cases, this chirotype can be very similar to the traditional one of the elemental, or basic, hand (**2**). Such hands have particularly high P factors (47) and much lower F factors, reflecting the broad palms and stubby fingers.

Earth hands are associated with practical, hard-working people who are very much down-to-earth in their outlook on life. To these people, the physical day-to-day realities of their life are more important than ideals, dreams and intellectual pursuits. They are reliable and honest people but can be overly conservative. Perhaps surprisingly, many musicians and artists have earth hands, which are ideal for the manual dexterity involved in playing a musical instrument or painting a work of art.

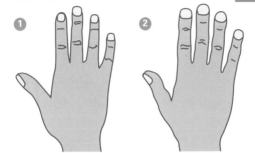

Fire hand (intuitive)

A long palm with relatively short fingers. An energetic, restless, individualistic nature. Fingertips can be rounded (**1**), spatulate (**2**), or square.

Fire hands indicate a charismatic, vibrant personality. Possessors of this cheirotype are born to lead, and they follow their ideas through with zeal and enthusiasm. Yet they are still practical, resourceful, and good at getting things done. They infect others with their zest, and love to be at the centre of attention. Fire hands reveal great energy, and those with this cheirotype are often physically active or athletic. They like to take risks and hate the petty details that bog down day-to-day matters. In fact, they are prone to boredom and frustration if they are not busy expressing themselves somehow.

 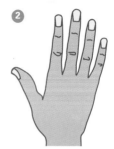

Water hand (sensitive)

A long palm with long fingers, tapering. Fingertips can be rounded (**1**) or pointed (**2**). These conic hand shapes are graceful and delicate, slender in shape and pleasing to the eye.

Water hands indicate an imaginative, emotional nature, often moody or introverted. The longer and leaner the fingers, the less down-to-earth the person is. Owners of water hands are not physically or emotionally strong, and they are prone to imagining slights and insults where none exist. Despite this tendency, many are in touch with their inner feelings and a few may even have particularly spiritual or even psychic. They can be preoccupied with ephemeral things such as fashion and beauty. They are not materialistic, however, just attracted to things of beauty. Perhaps surprisingly, they can also be patient and gentle people, well suited to caring professions.

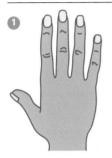 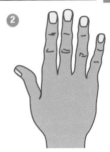

Air hand (intellectual)

Like the earth hand, the air hand has a square palm. The key difference between the two types is the presence of relatively long fingers. Fingers can be smooth (**1**) or knotted (**2**). Fingertips are usually rounded or conic though they may also be spatulate.

> Air hands reveal a clever, rational, articulate nature, both aware and orderly (sometimes too orderly perhaps). The square palm reveals that they have a practical side, and the long fingers reveal their creative side. Possessors of such hands are renowned for their ability to put their ideas to use and pursue their ambitions to fruition. They expend a lot of their energies in intellectual rather than physical activities and can have a tendency to neglect or over-analyze their emotional life.

PERCUSSION AND THE CURVE OF CREATIVITY

In palmistry, the percussion is that edge of the palm that lies on the opposite side to the thumb. In order to be able to analyze a person's percussion (as well as other factors such as joint shape) from a print, you will need to draw an outline around the hand before it is lifted off the paper. When taking or outlining a print, however, put as little pressure as possible on this soft area to prevent squashing it out of shape.

The Mount of the Moon (imaginative intelligence), Upper mount of Mars (capacity to act) and the Mount of Mercury (intellectual energies) are located in the percussion. For this reason, the shape and curve of the percussion reveals how a person shapes and channels their creative energies and intuitive powers. This curve is often called the curve of creativity. The most important aspect of the curve is its summit.

Curve of creativity

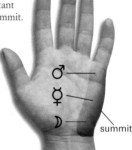

▬	percussion
☽	Mount of the Moon
♂	Upper mount of Mars
☿	Mount of Mercury

summit

POSITION OF SUMMIT

Summit in the Moon Strength and energy take a physical form. The higher the summit gets, the more the balance there is between physical strength and strength of character. These people have endurance and are authoritative but they possess an underdeveloped sense of judgment and can lack the energy to complete tasks.

Summit in Mars There is a balance between physical strength and strength of character (the best balance is exactly between the Mount of the Moon and the Upper mount of Mars).

Summit in Mercury Indicates a psychic individual or one who lives in a fantasy world. These people are often impractical, intellectually creative, with forceful personality but weak physically.

Straight percussion People with no summits are rare types with little interest in creative matters or subconscious drives.

Position of summit

Physical strength
The lower the summit, the greater the subject's physical strength.

Psychic strength and strength of character
The higher the summit, the greater the subject's psychic strength.

COMPATIBILITY AND HAND SHAPE

Palmistry can be used to work out how compatible people are, bearing in mind that the compatibility of two people is not just based on what they have in common with each other. There is much more to a long-lasting relationship than having interests in common; sometimes it is the differences that help keep people together as well as their particular approaches to life and love.

Comparing and analyzing people's hand shapes, mounts and lines can reveal the ways in which the two halves of a couple both think alike and how they differ from, or complement, each other. Are they flexible and open-minded enough to cope with the differences, even seeing them as positive? A careful hand reading, or two, will reveal the answer to such questions.

If you are carrying out compatibility readings for anyone other than yourself and your partner, remember that such readings need palmists to be even more sensitive than normal: phrase potentially negative findings in a positive way if at all possible, and take care not to ring the death knell on any relationship. Make clear any differences that could damage the relationship by all means, but always mention any positive things that you pick up.

The table on the opposite page gives brief snapshots of compatibilities between different hand shapes; read the more detailed analyses that follow for further information.

HAND SHAPE	Fire	Water	Earth	Air
Fire	A fiery match full of passion that may, however, burn out too soon	Both are passionate in different ways, so the match could work	Earth gives Fire stability but match may never happen if sparks don't fly at first	Will need great effort to work: Fire will need to control jealousy
Water	Water is happy for Fire to take the lead but might dampen Fire's spirit	A perfect match that may not last in the real world if both are too sensitive	Not a good match: Water's sensitivity will overwhelm Earth	Could work if they share creative pursuits but Water may be too sulky for Air
Earth	Fire can bring Earth to life with passion, but it may not be reciprocated	Not a good match: Earth is frustrated by Water's illogical nature	Solid and lasting but likely to be dull	Difficult: Earth is unable to express feelings while Air is unwilling to
Air	Needs effort to work: Air will need to express feelings to Fire	Might work as Air could put Water's intuitive abilities to creative use	Difficult: Earth is inflexible while Air is ever-changing	Well-suited but match will be cool rather than passionate

Fire with Fire As would be expected from the pairing of two such passionate and charismatic people, any union between the owners of fire hands will not lack excitement.

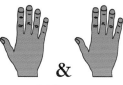

The difficulties may lie in the partners' ability to compromise. Fire hands indicate the ability and, more importantly in relationship terms, the desire to lead. Two people straining to take the lead in a personal relationship can spell disaster unless they can work out some basic compromises and learn to respect each other's needs and wishes for the limelight; otherwise they will soon tire of the relationship.

Fire with Water In their own way, owners of Water hands are just as passionate as Fire types. Their passion takes a more obsessive and inward-

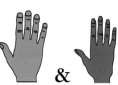

looking direction though. Water will be happy for Fire to take the lead, but Water may turn out to be just as controlling as Fire by using moods, silences and sulks to control situations; this sort of underhand manipulation can put Fire types off. However, watery types can provide the inspiration to fuel Fire's passions, and if the two can be attentive to their differences, the relationship could work out very well.

Fire with Earth Partners with these two hand shapes are very different types of people: their very differences could make the relationship work though. Earth can help calm Fire 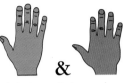 down, making them focus on their aims and what needs to be done to achieve them, not forgetting those petty details that Fire types normally neglect. In return, Fire could inspire Earth types to take a few risks and broaden their horizons somewhat. Perhaps the largest hurdle to the relationship, however, will be whether the two will see enough in the other to attract them in the first place.

Fire with Air The differences in approach to life between these two are quite fundamental: Fire types are direct, open, unafraid of showing their enthusiasm and materially 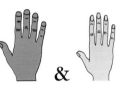 ambitious; Air types prefer a more cloistered existence pursuing intellectual gratifications. Having said that, Fire's passionate declarations of love can put Air's tendency to over-analyze relationships to rest, and Air's high-achieving nature will win Fire's respect. As with all hand readings, look at other aspects such as the development of mounts and appearance of lines to get a better idea of whether the relationship will work or not.

Water with Water Water types are ideally suited to each other. They understand perfectly the other's sensitivities and will hopefully be sympathetic enough to take care not to

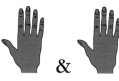

cause hurt by thoughtless remarks. If communication ever breaks down, however, their relationship could become blighted by misunderstandings and misinterpretations of the other's naturally introspective moods. Water types can be very aware of their emotions and in touch with their feelings, and these attributes help make any relationship work better, and this is particularly true if both members of a couple show this awareness.

Water with Earth This match has the potential to be another example of chalk and cheese *not* working. Water hand types typically being very sensitive people while Earth hand types are

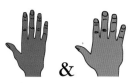

often accused of insensitivity, it is hard to see how two such opposites would get along. Look for mitigating signs on the hands – such as a strong headline on the Water hand, which would make the person more down-to-earth than normal – that might make the difference between the relationship lasting or failing. On a more positive note, Earth's practical nature could combine with Water's creativity to make something special.

Water with Air Water and Air are similar in many ways, their favourite pursuits are more intellectual or aesthetic rather than materialistic, and they can both be 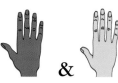 creative and inspired thinkers. Air may not be sensitive enough at times to Water's needs, however, and will either find Water's moods exasperating or won't even notice them. Air will be inspired by Water's intuitive and at times psychic abilities, and the two could definitely have a fruitful creative partnership if not a trouble-free relationship.

Earth with Earth In this case, like does attract like. Two Earth types can easily get along; they will not find the other's reluctance to express feelings unusual, and if living together, their 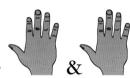 shared lives will soon take on a comfortable routine. The union could become dull and unstimulating, however, but this may be more noticeable to onlookers than the two members of the couple themselves, who value security and stability (and regular sexual gratification!) more than excitement. Their practical, hardworking abilities will mean the likelihood of a comfortable life together, well supplied with material possessions, which are often important to people with this hand shape.

Earth with Air Both Air and Air and Earth are practical types, but this is about all they will have in common. While Earth's ambitions are typically more 'down-to-Earth', Air will be 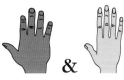 building ivory towers in the sky. They may find that this fundamentally different approach to life shatters their chances of a happy relationship. Again, before declaring the relationship a no-hoper, look for mitigating signs: if Air has full long and thick basal phalanges (the bottom section of the fingers), for instance, then the two may have more in common than otherwise since this indicates an interest in more Earthy pursuits.

Air with Air Two Air types are likely to get on very well together. Of course, they share the same interests, and the fact that neither will be overly possessive or otherwise 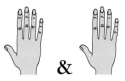 emotionally demanding can only help to further prolong any relationship between two Air types. A couple made up of two such people will be comfortable but cool rather than passionate. The most frequent late-night pursuit is likely to be lingering conversation or intellectual theorizing, with which both will be more than happy.

HEALTH AND HAND SHAPE

Hand shape on its own is unlikely to be very revealing about specific illnesses, but it can reveal the tendency, or likelihood, of certain health problems arising. Always look for other signs on the hand, and never diagnose health matters unless you are very confident in your abilities.

	Strengths	Weaknesses
Fire	• very energetic (needs to do a lot of sport to vent excess energy)	• disorders of the circulatory system • overwork, causing stress and burn-out
Water	• able to use intuitive powers and knowledge of inner mind to help heal themselves and ward off illnesses	• prone to addictions • has a tendency to worry that, at times of great stress, can lead to nervous breakdown
Earth	• usually enjoys basic good health throughout much of early life • athletic, and has great stamina if not speed	• tendency to depression and heart or bowel problems in later life • watch out for accidents at work
Air	• energetic • health should be resilient if plenty of time to relax is taken	• nervous tension • respiratory problems

CAREER AND HAND SHAPE

Just by looking at the shape of someone's hands you can begin to formulate opinions on their abilities in the work environment and even pick out suitable occupations.

FIRE AT WORK

Abilities and weaknesses

- good at motivating and influencing others
- able to lead but may not take direction well themselves
- enjoys challenge and thrives on stress
- works best with a good personal assistant to take care of the day-to-day details of carrying out plans; an aspect

that Fire-hand types tend to ignore (since they prefer to see wood and not the trees).

- an inspired orator
- resourceful
- not afraid of taking risks

Suitable occupations

- actor
- advertising executive
- architect
- athlete
- barrister
- broadcaster
- entrepreneur, or otherwise self-employed
- journalist
- manager, but preferably managing director
- mountaineer
- politician
- officer in armed forces or police force
- salesperson
- something in public relations

EARTH AT WORK

Abilities and weaknesses

- best suited to working outdoors
- practical
- hardworking
- conservative and inflexible, and doesn't like change: therefore Earth-hand types should regularly review their skills and make sure to take up any training courses on offer
- has green fingers
- in-touch with nature
- lacks imagination
- not always good at dealing with others on a one-to-one basis but will work well in a team, regularly taking on the tasks others disdain
- good with hands, including technically skilled work such as playing a musical instrument
- will excel at physically demanding work

Suitable occupations

- animal breeder
- artist
- boxer
- builder
- cook
- craft worker
- engineer
- farmer
- fisherman
- gardener
- horticulturist
- mason
- mechanic
- miner
- musician
- park-keeper
- potter
- sculptor
- veterinary surgeon
- zookeeper

WATER AT WORK

Abilities and weaknesses

- caring and sensitive to others' needs, and able to empathize
- creative and intuitive
- easily picks up on latest fashions and trends, and intuitively understands mood of public feeling
- able to express themselves
- not capable of physically demanding roles
- interested in the arts
- like to be able to express themselves
- not very organized and tends to have poor management skills
- fashion editor
- flexible

Suitable occupations

- actor
- artist
- beautician
- charity worker, or volunteer
- child carer
- clairvoyant
- counsellor
- doctor
- fashion designer
- fashion editor
- fashion model
- interior designer
- lifestyle journalist
- make-up artist
- member of clergy
- nurse
- nursery teacher
- palmist
- poet
- practitioner of complementary medicine
- researcher
- social worker
- something in public relations
- spiritualist
- therapist
- writer

AIR AT WORK

Abilities and weaknesses

- natural affinity for all sciences, especially physics, and mathematics
- logical
- articulate
- organized
- intelligent and intellectual
- has a practical streak
- creative
- able to plan and carry out complex tasks
- enjoys the communication of ideas
- not always easy to work with as can be brusque and unsympathetic
- fascinated by the realm of ideas
- needs a mentally rewarding job

Suitable occupations

- aeronautic engineer
- architect
- civil engineer
- computer programmer
- critic
- detective
- town planner
- electrician, or electronics expert
- essayist
- graphic designer
- information technologist
- inventor
- journalist
- mechanic
- nonfiction editor
- philosopher
- playwright
- polemicist
- politician
- scientist
- something in the travel industry
- statistician
- teacher or professor
- theologian
- tv producer
- website designer

GENERAL HAND FEATURES

Whichever classification system you use, however, it will give you nothing more than a few initial hints, general pointers to start off your overall reading. Further pointers can be found in the size and texture of the skin of your subject's hand. Someone whose hand is small in comparison to the rest of their build will think and act on a large scale, behaving decisively and leaving the detail to others. Proportionately large hands indicate a thoughtful, patient mind and – surprising as it may seem – a skill with fine, delicate, detailed work.

A palm with a firm and elastic texture usually belongs to an optimistic, healthy person; a soft, flabby and fleshy palm indicates sensuality and indolence; and a hard, dry, wooden palm a tense, chronic worrier. So, as you begin your reading, carefully consider the hand as a whole before going on to look in detail at the fingers, mounts and lines. If you intend to work from a hand print, remember to take a good look at the whole hand as you make the print!

SKIN TEXTURE

People with fine, smooth skin texture tend to be emotional and sensitive to their surroundings, especially so if they have Water shape hands. Those with with rougher, coarser hands are less sensitive and have a more take it or leave it approach to life. This skin type is often associated with Earth hands. While it is true that these people can be callous and aggressive, don't forget to look for other signs in the hand that may balance these tendencies before announcing the presence of such negative traits.

Compare the skin texture of the back of the hand to that of the palm. The palm reveals the inner person, while the back of the hand reveals the more public persona.

fine skin texture   coarse skin texture

HAIRINESS

Noticeable hair on the back of the hands is a largely male trait, and hairy hands on either sex can denote supposedly masculine characteristics such as aggression, vitality and even cruelty. Fine hair can be attributed to people of faint disposition – generally the coarser the hair, the more physical the person. People with no hair on their hands can be refined but cowardly, while hair on the hands can denote inconsistency. Hair on the thumb in particular can reveal a vivid imagination; hair on the backs of fingers reveals a strong ambition.

HAND SPAN AND POSITION

Fingers held stiffly together (a) Cautious, suspicious and unsociable.

Evenly spaced fingers (b) A well-balanced mind, likely to be successful in any field.

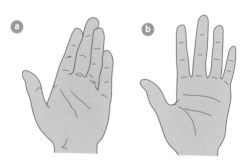

Well-separated fingers Independent and freedom-loving.

Wide gap between all fingers Frank, open and trusting –
an almost child-like nature.

Widest space between thumb and first finger Outgoing, a
generous disposition.

Widest space between first and second fingers Not easily
influenced by others, independent in thought and action.

Widest space between second and third fingers Free from
anxieties for the future, light-hearted.

Widest space between third and fourth fingers (c) An
independent and original thinker.

Fourth finger very separated from the other fingers (d)
Difficulties in personal relationships, isolated and
alienated.

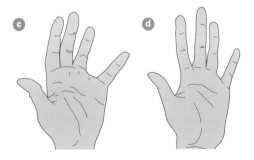

3. Fingers and the Thumb

Nearly all doctors inspect a patient's fingertips when making an examination, as the nails give important indications of a person's state of health. And just as we usually accept that people who bite their nails tend to be tense and anxious, so the shape and colour of the nails can give us hints to the character of their owner.

Palmists look too at the shape of the fingers, their flexibility and their position on the hand in relation to one

FLEXIBILITY AND BEND OF THE FINGERS

To assess the flexibility of a person's fingers and hands, ask them to hold their right hand in front of them with the fingers pointing down and the palm facing out. Then, using their left hand, they should gently push the fingers back towards the body as far as they will naturally go. The degree by which the hand and fingers are able to bend is a measure of the hand's suppleness.

stiff

another. They also read much into the separate segments or 'phalanges'. So, as always, you should remember to take the overall view. For example, in a square, smooth-jointed finger, the reflective qualities of the square shape will balance the impulsive nature shown by the smooth joints, and indicate a person of good intuition. But in a pointed, smooth-jointed finger we have a double indication of impulsiveness – quite possibly a person who never looks before he leaps.

normal

supple

In general, when assessing flexibility, the rule is that the more flexible the hand, the more flexible and easy going the person. People with very supple hands are imaginative and can even be accused of being dreamers.

Stiff hands are thought to indicate stiff, rigid and unyielding people who are both stubborn and unreceptive. Truly stiff hands occur rarely, however, and in reality few people are that uncompromising.

Flexibility can also be an indicator of the how energetic a person is. Hands that offer little resistance to being pushed back on themselves can indicate a weak personality, someone without the ability or temper to put their ideas into action. Hands that are flexible but 'springy', offering resistance to pressure, are said to be elastic. People with elastic hands are energetic and active, well able to channel their energies constructively.

Whether the fingers are curved or straight is also important:

Curved fingers bending slightly towards the palm A prudent and acquisitive nature.

Curved and stiff fingers Fearful, cautious, narrow-minded, tenacious.

Curved fingers, bending away from the palm Someone who ignores rules and regulations, who is chatty and good company.

Backward curving and supple fingers An open mind, inquisitive, attractive.

JOINTS

The shape of the finger joints can be very revealing of a person's character. Do not be misled into thinking that the sort of job a person does determines whether or not they have noticeable joints. Joint shape is determined by genetics not experience. While some diseases such as rheumatism and arthritis can affect the shape of a person's finger joints, generally the joints on a person's hand are little affected by factors such as whether or not they engage in hard manual labour.

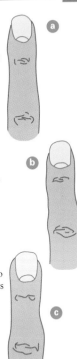

Puffy joints Reveal a hedonistic, pleasure-loving person.

Smooth joints (a) A quick-thinking, impulsive, inspired extrovert, not very analytical or logical. Typically with Water or Air shape hands, but with square hand can indicate someone who will jump to conclusions. Smooth joints on conical hand types belong to very intuitive characters.

Knotty joints (b) A deep-thinking, dignified introvert who is analytical and critical but not very friendly.

Large joints (c) Methodical, rational.

LENGTH AND WIDTH

To assess finger length, measure the length of the palm, from wrist to base of fingers (**P**), and the length of middle finger from base to tip (**F**).

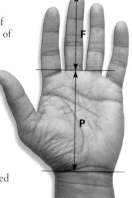

If F is less than 80 percent of P (i.e., less than F x 0.8), then the fingers are short. If F is more than 80 percent of P, then the fingers are long.

The length of a person's fingers should be considered along with finger width.

SHORT FINGERS

Short fingers (**a**) are often found on square and Earth or Fire shape hands. Short fingers are generally associated with impulsiveness and intuition. These people can seem organized and are good at getting things going, but they are easily bored by details, and this can let them down. They are quick to pass judgment, but do not consider the ramifications of their decisions too closely.

Short and fat Impulsive, hasty, not very intelligent and perhaps selfish. These people lack ideals and place a high value on the material aspects of life.

Short and thin The owner of such fingers will do well in life. These people are responsible, well-suited to lead, and unafraid of decision making.

LONG FINGERS

While those with short fingers are good at seeing the wood but not the trees, the reverse is true of those with long fingers (**b**). They take a much more particular view of life, interested in the details and peculiarities of their surroundings.

Long and thin Denote intelligent, idealistic, imaginative superficial and impractical people.

Long and fat These are the fingers of a poet or visionary.

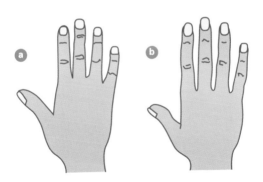

LENGTH, WIDTH AND COMPATIBILITY

Consult this table to see how well people with fingers of different lengths and widths will get on.

	Long & thin	Long & fat	Short & thin	Short & fat
Long & thin	these two will love the idea of each other but this might not last a long time	the one with the thinner fingers is exactly how their partner would like to be seen	these two will get on very well and will bring out the best in each other	the shorter-fingered one is canny enough to romance the other, if interested
Long & fat	the one with the thinner fingers will feel obliged to compete, and is likely to fail	unlikely to last: each really needs a more down-to-earth partner for stability	could be perfect: the shorter-fingered one will support the visionary in their aims	these two inhabit different worlds and are unlikely to be able to ever get on
Short & thin	the short-fingered one will help their partner realize their dreams	will last as long as the one with thinner fingers is ok with second place	this couple will be passionate but they are prone to fight too much	the thinner-fingered partner will tire of the other's lazy and selfish nature
Short & fat	the greater the length difference, the less likely they are to get along	one is inspired by material gain, the other by spiritual matters	the fatter-fingered one will be happy to let the other provide for their needs	well-suited if each can bear to see their own faults in their partner

LENGTH, WIDTH AND CAREER

Consult this table to assess the working abilities of people according to the length and width of their fingers.

	Weaknesses & strengths	Suitable occupations
Long & thin	• pays attention to detail • takes great care over their work • is very thorough • can work too slowly • clever but not intuitive	• musician • artist • anything that requires good hand–eye coordination • project manager • copy-editor
Long & fat	• very creative • able to manipulate people, both wisely and unwisely • highly intelligent • likely to be at the cutting edge of their profession	• political leader • religious leader • poet • playwright • inventor • seer • publisher
Short & thin	• able to pick up new skills very quickly • capable of inspired thought • doesn't pay enough attention to detail • good in steering roles	• company founder • city trader or financial analyst • any higher management position • high-level politician or civil servant
Short & fat	• ambitious for material rewards • lacks determination to improve skills • lacks patience • is not reliable	• salesperson, or other commission-based work • largely destined for mundane work unless a concerted effort is made to tackle training

FINGERTIP SHAPE

The shape of the fingertip is just as important as the length of the finger. Indeed the two factors should be considered together. The fingertips comprise the top phalange of each finger, and there are five main shapes it can take: square, spatulate, pointed, conical and rounded. A person can have more than one type of fingertip on a hand. If this is the case, read the sections on individual fingers to find out what the different meanings the presence of each finger tip has for each finger.

Square (a) Square fingertips have blunt ends with little or no rounding. Square fingertips indicate a practical and common sensical nature. They are typically found on short fingers, in which case they stress the thoughtful and cautious aspects of a person's nature. On long fingers, square fingertips help ground the owner's psychic and intuitive energies.

Spatulate (b) Spatulate fingertips are recognizable because the tip is wider than the top joint on the finger. The presence of these fingertips indicate and independent, original, energetic person. On long fingers, spatulate fingertips are likely to reveal musical abilities. Successful scientists and inventors often have short fingers with spatulate tips.

Pointed (c) Pointed fingertips are often found at the ends of long, tapered fingers. On such fingers they denote an impulsive, artistic but punctilious character. These fingertips enhance the person's spirituality and refinement but can also exacerbate their superficial tendencies. On short fingers, however, they can reveal and perhaps even channel a hidden spirituality.

Conical (d) Conical fingertips are like pointed fingertips with the tips cut off, leaving a rounded or blunt tip on the otherwise tapered finger. The possessors of such fingertips are often highly successful people, entrepreneurs, artists or musicians.

Rounded (e) Rounded fingers are the most common variation. They are indicative of a straightforward nature. The rule is that they can have a balancing effect on other attributes, in particular those denoted by finger length. So, on long fingers they can serve to bring an element of practicality to the person's otherwise high-flown character. On short fingers, they can temper the person's material ambitions with a more intellectual slant.

FINGERTIP SHAPE AND COMPATIBILITY

Consult this table to see how well people with fingertips of different shapes are likely to get on.

	Square	Spatulate	Pointed	Conical	Rounded
Square	a solid but perhaps dull match	spatulate one will inject life into their partner	square one might 'ground' the other	chalk and cheese that just might get on	this could improve squares if they don't resist
Spatulate	spatulate one may tire of partner	an exciting and busy couple with lots to say	spatulate one may be too free-spirited	sparks will fly but it will be passionate	sparks are unlikely to fly
Pointed	they have little in common and will soon tire	if both are artistic, they will get on	romantics: too sensitive for each other	conical one will enjoy partner's refinement	rounded one will be taken for granted
Conical	square's practical abilities channel conical's talents	well-suited dynamic couple	pointed one will enjoy the attention given	emotion-ally secure couple	rounded one will stabilize conical one
Rounded	both need a more lively partner to shine	rounded one may be too tame for partner	neither will sweep the other off their feet	both will benefit from the differences	peaceful, loving couple

FINGERTIP SHAPE AND CAREER
Consult this table to judge the working abilities of people according to the shape of their fingertips.

	Weaknesses & strengths	Suitable occupations
Square	<ul><li>practical</li><li>careful</li><li>methodical</li><li>logical but not inspired thinker</li></ul>	<ul><li>mechanic</li><li>engineer</li><li>technician</li><li>clerk, or office administrator</li></ul>
Spatulate	<ul><li>an original thinker</li><li>creative</li><li>if combined with knotty joints: an intellectual with radical ideas</li></ul>	<ul><li>likely to be a pioneer in their chosen profession</li><li>inventor</li><li>explorer</li><li>professor</li></ul>
Pointed	<ul><li>artistic talents</li><li>strongly imaginative</li><li>can lack a sense of purpose at work if not allowed to be creative</li></ul>	<ul><li>writer</li><li>poet</li><li>theoretician</li><li>advertising executive</li><li>fashion designer</li></ul>
Conical	<ul><li>able to combine practical and creative abilities</li><li>flexible</li><li>job security is important to them</li></ul>	<ul><li>computer-game designer, or any other type of creative–IT worker</li><li>graphic designer</li><li>successful business person</li></ul>
Rounded	<ul><li>an average achiever</li><li>can lack ambition</li><li>needs committed coaching to excel</li><li>diligent</li></ul>	<ul><li>people with rounded fingertips are flexible, and this trait reveals no particular aptitudes for any job on its own</li></ul>

DROPS OF WATER

One feature in particular on a person's fingertips can be very revealing. It is the drop of water. The underside of most fingertips are smooth and rounded or even flat. On some hands, however, the underside of one or more fingertips has what looks like a drop of water about to fall.

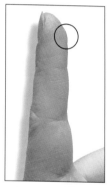

The presence of drops of water reveal a person with a very tactile nature. Even one drop of water can denote a love of textures if nothing else. The peaked fleshy pads give the possessor exceptionally sensitive fingertips, allowing them to gather a great deal of information about something through touch alone. Some would even claim the presence of many drops of water give that person supernatural abilities to intuit information from touch alone.

FINGERPRINTS

The study of the ridge patterns on fingertips is called dermatoglyphics. Fingerprint patterns are established about 18 weeks after conception. Unlike the other lines on the hand, from then on they are fixed and unchanging. This, as we know, makes them very useful in the detection of criminals, but they can also be useful in the detection of personality. When more than one type of fingerprint pattern appears in a hand, their different characteristics will be blended in the personality. The number of fingers involved can give us an indication of the balance of that blend: a person with several fingers showing tented arches is likely to be considerably more stubborn than a person with just one.

There are three basic types of fingerprint: the loop, the whorl and the arch, with variations existing on each type. A person can have more than one type of fingerprint so you should assess which is the dominant type. The more a certain pattern recurs, the more emphasis is placed on the trait it indicates.

Also, analyze each finger separately since the finger a pattern appears on can have implications for the overall meaning. The position of the fingerprint pattern on the finger is also important. If the heart of the pattern appears above the centre of the phalange, then the energy expresses is more intellectual than practical. The lower down it is, the more the reverse is true.

THE ARCH

A Basic arch This fingerprint indicates a practical and materialistic nature. People with arches as fingerprints are reserved but hardworking. They can be hard-hearted, insensitive, sceptical and unemotional. On the index and middle finger, arches can reveal an inability to express oneself.

B Tented arch Recognizable for the so-called 'tent pole' that props the arch up. While they are similar in other respects to those who have basic arches, they are more impulsive and emotional. The possessors of such fingerprints are highly strung, artistic and obsessive – but stubborn.

THE LOOP

C Basic (or ulna) loop This is the most common fingerprint pattern. Basic loops point towards the thumb, with their base, or starting point, at the percussion side of the hand. People who have such fingerprints on their hands are generally mild-tempered and straightforward, with a quick, lively and versatile mind.

D Reverse (or radial) loop These loops are like basic loops, but they start and finish in the opposite direction. Owners share the same personality characteristics as those of basic loops, but they are more confident and less afraid to speak their mind. Reverse loops are far less common than basic loops.

THE WHORL

E Spiral whorl People who have spiral whorls as their fingerprints are individualists with a strong, definite personalities. Potentially brilliant, they work best when self-employed. They can be inflexible and take time to make decisions, however, since they prefer to have ample time to reflect on matters.

F Concentric whorl This fingerprint is a series of complete circles within each other. It is a much rarer pattern than the spiral whorl, but the characteristics it indicates are very similar. It is most commonly found on the index or ring fingers. A person with 10 such prints will have great potential but can be prone to stress.

G COMPOSITE

Composite fingerprints look like two
loops pulling in opposite directions.
Often, they can look like the ancient
Chinese yin–yang symbol. While
these people are open-minded and
able to sympathize with others, they
can be indecisive and even muddle-
headed personalities.

H PEACOCK'S EYE

The peacock's eye fingerprint looks
like a loop at first glance. On closer
inspection, however, you will see a
whorl at the heart of the loop, like the
eye on a peacock's tail. This
fingerprint is very favourable,
denoting as it does good luck and
conferring protection on its owner.

I TRI RADIUS

If you have any difficulty in
differentiating one type of fingerprint
pattern from another, look for the
tri-radius. The presence, absence or
number of this triangular shape
identifies the fingerprint pattern. An
arch print does not have a tri-radus, a
loop print has one and a whorl has
two tri-radii.

FINGERPRINTS AND COMPATIBILITY

Consult this table to see how well people with fingertips of different shapes are likely to get on.

	Basic arch	Tented arch	Basic loop	Reverse loop
Basic arch	a good solid match but perhaps dull	a loyal and affectionate couple	might work, but they need to talk more	likely to clash over something
Tented arch	compatible as they share interests	a solid but lively relationship	differences will bring out the best	both are outspoken and stubborn
Basic loop	one with arch needs to lighten up	one with the arch may be too jealous	a fun, good-humoured pair	a mutually rewarding relationship
Reverse loop	these two have little in common	likely to fight often but will stick together	both like to remain independent	a lively good-natured but flighty pair
Spiral whorl	both like to get their own way	both are stubborn: they will fight	a match that gets better with time	unique pairing of individualists
Concentric whorl	the arch is too dull for the whorl	will work if the one with whorl leads	one with loop is too quiet for the other	equally matched but fiery couple
Composite	relationship will be hard work	the one with the arch will rule the roost	a relaxed and friendly pairing	differences will bring out the best
Peacock's eye	dissimilar people but it could work	the one with arch will idolize the other	contented rather than passionate	a perfect match

	Spiral whorl	Concentric whorl	Composite	Peacock's eye
Basic arch	unlikely to get along as each is too strong-willed	whorled one worries too much for the other	not well-suited unless particularly tolerant	can probably overcome any difficulties they have
Tented arch	emotionally draining match for both	both prone to stress, so match may be fraught	composite is likely to be unhappy with partner	partner with eye will love the other less
Basic loop	one with loop will take second place	not well-suited but exciting for one with loop	tie is not strong so one may wander	contented rather than passionate
Reverse loop	will fight at first then fall in love	can achieve great heights together	one with loop able to make partner feel secure	very happy together and supportive of each other
Spiral whorl	fiery but very passionate couple	may be too alike to get along	composite is happy if partner takes the lead	one with eye needs to have high stress tolerance
Concentric whorl	love, or hate, at first sight is likely	committed to, but overly analytical of, each other	composite miserable with difficult partner	well-suited: both excel at anything they do
Composite	one partner needs to take charge	on e with whorl needs to be more sympathetic	an easy-going and peace-loving couple	unlikely to get together, but works if they do
Peacock's eye	a very fortuitous pairing	life together will be an adventure	a happy if uneventful match	soulmates: a match made in heaven

FINGERPRINTS AND CAREER

Consult this table to judge the working abilities and of people according to their dominant fingerprint type.

	Weaknesses & strengths	Suitable occupations
Basic arch	• is very practical • hard-working • not particularly good at teamwork • dependable and loyal • can be resistant to change and new technology	• anything that involves manual dexterity: • builder • painter • surgeon • musician • labourer
Tented arch	• is very practical • hard-working • creative • artistic • can be resistant to change and new technology	• musician • artist • sculptor • surgeon • museum curator
Basic loop	• well-suited to teamwork • enjoys, and needs, variety at work • flexible • finds it difficult to assert themselves and supervise others effectively	• committee worker • graphic designer • journalist • temporary work • court reporter
Reverse loop	• well-suited to teamwork • needs constant stimulation to remain motivated: has no patience for repetitive or mundane tasks • flexible • good with people	• personal assistant to a high-level executive • television researcher • personnel manager • public relations

	Weaknesses & strengths	Suitable occupations
Spiral whorl	• well-suited to working alone or being self-employed • can appear to be not very decisive as their analytical minds need to assess the ins and outs of every decision	• business entrepreneur, particularly in the field of information technology • for example, founder of internet start-up company • academic • scientist
Concentric whorl	• likes to be in charge • responsible • the more such fingerprints the person has, the greater the expertise they will accumulate in their chosen profession	• middle-level to high-level management • financial analyst • economist • consultant physician
Composite	• very good at seeing both sides of a story • impartial • objective • can be resistant to change and new technology though	• mediator • referee • counsellor • judge or magistrate • diplomat • negotiator • careers advisor • social worker
Peacock's eye	• will be fortunate in any undertaking • flexible and adaptable, these people are not afraid of change • finds it easy to get on with colleagues	• people with this fingerprint should capitalize on their innate luckiness, take a few risks, and perhaps even go into business on their own, whatever their profession

THE SET OF THE FINGERS

The point at which the fingers join the palm is called the arc. Inspecting the arc on a hand reveals whether fingers are evenly set or unevenly set, creating either a disjointed line or a smooth line or curve. When assessing whether or not a person's fingers are set low or high, the middle finger is used as the baseline. In other words, this finger is never set low, but decides the level for the other fingers.

EVENLY SET FINGERS

1 Level set When fingers are level set, the arc is a straight line. Such arcs are uncommon, and they reveal a very strong character. A confident and assured but intolerant person with plenty of ambition and drive, one who will do well in life.

middle finger

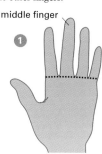

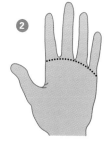

2 Arched set When fingers are set in an arch, the arc is a smooth curve. Also called the Roman arc, this is the most common set. These people have a positive, broad outlook on life, and are friendly and reliable. Not particularly imaginative but willing to accept change.

UNEVENLY SET FINGERS

In general, fingers that are unevenly set do not indicate positive traits. Which particular negative trait is indicated is determined by which finger is set lowest since each finger is associated with particular personality traits. Sometimes, though, people can defeat their doubts or inadequacies and achieve success if they expend a great deal of energy.

1 Index (first) finger
2 Middle (second) finger
3 Ring (third) finger
4 Little (fourth) finger

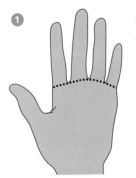

1 Index finger is lowest

The index finger is associated with ego and ambition. A person with a low-set index finger will have tendencies to be shy and unassertive, someone who inwardly feels inferior to everyone else. They lack leadership qualities and can behave unpredictably. Remember to consider the overall length of the finger as well as set, however.

2 Ring finger is lowest A person with a low-set ring finger is likely to be frustrated in career matters, one who has had to take a job contrary to real talents and inclinations. This finger is related to the realm of sense of well-being and creative fulfilment, so perhaps the subject needs to work more creatively to realize their true occupation in which they will be happy and fulfilled.

3 Little finger is lowest This finger is related to the realm of communications, and a low-set example indicates an inquiring mind but nothing comes easily for these people, and they will have to struggle hard to succeed. Other potential problems include a lack of self-confidence. A low-set little finger, however, is not all bad. It can indicate an aptitude for physics, chemistry and medicine, probably due in part to the owner's inquiring mind.

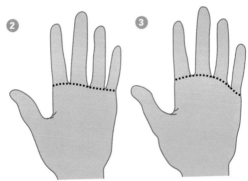

FINGERNAILS

Nearly all doctors inspect a patient's fingertips when
making an examination, as the nails give important
indications of a person's state of health. And just as we
usually accept that people who bite their nails tend to be
tense and anxious, so the shape and colour of the nails can
give us hints to the character of their owner.

NAIL SHAPE

1 Short nails (unbitten) Energetic and curious people
tend to have short nails. They are intuitive but temper this
with logic.

2 Short nails (unbitten), broader than they are long
Critical and quick-tempered, people with broad nails tend
to be rash and insensitive. As well as being unsympathetic
to others, they are also critical of themselves but will not
hold a grudge against someone.

3 Broad, long nails, rounded at the tip A person of sound
judgement who is capable of clear thinking. Broad-minded
and non-critical, these people are open to new ideas. They
can have tendency to be more intuitive than practical.

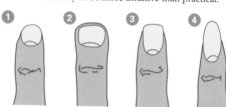

4 Long, almond-shaped nails A placid and easy-going person, a dreamer with an artistic streak. These nails can also indicate a tendency to sulk when offended.

5 Very large, square nails An even, placid character with a robust personality and a practical streak. These people are well suited to both manual work and the planning of large complex projects.

6 Fan-shaped nails In which nails are shaped like an open fan: much broader at the top than at the base. This indicates a sensitive nature, and the owner may well be prone to stress. They are active and dynamic, though, but run on nervous energy and are therefore prone to stress.

7 Wrap-around, or Hippocratic, nails Recognizable for the way the nail bulges when seen in profile, this shape denotes a bright, intelligent and lively character who is inclined to obesity and respiratory problems.

8 Convex, or spoon-shaped, nails When viewed from the side, such nails appear to be dented. The owners of such fingernails are overly sensitive and tend to bottle things up.

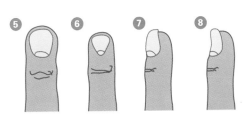

NAIL COLOUR

Nail colour is thought to be particularly revealing of sexual energy.

White Cold and conceited, these people tend to be unhappy but calm. They are selfish lovers and show little passion towards others.

Pink A person with a warm and outgoing nature, good health, and good nature have pink nails. These people have reached a good balance between the physical and emotional aspects of their sex life.

Pale Nails with little colour indicate a lack of vitality and a cold and selfish nature. These people lack sexual vitality and have a correspondingly low sex drive.

Red A violent temper combined with a strong and passionate sex drive. People with red nails are best able to express their emotions physically. They have large amounts of energy, which, if not channelled constructively, can become destructive.

Bluish Generally an unhealthy sign. In people with no circulatory problems, blue nails indicate a cold and reserved nature, perhaps someone with considerable sexual inhibitions. Check for other signs on the hand that point towards introversion to see how far these inhibitions go.

NAIL HEALTH

While certain features on a hand can indicate medical complaints, and this is especially true of nails, try to avoid giving a diagnosis of a particular illness or condition unless you are medically qualified to do so. Also, because of the time it takes to grow nails (six months from quick to fingertip), indicators can sometimes reveal past states rather than present conditions.

1 Speckles White spots on nails show a person is tired and run down. Take a holiday!

2 Vertical ridges Nervous, tense, prone to rheumatism and back problems.

3 Splinters Possible heart problems.

4 Horizontal ridges If flat when viewed from the side, the lines indicate that a person has suffered from a fever in past months. If markedly furrowed when seen from the side, the lines can reflect some relatively recent emotional trauma.

5 Moons The moon is the whitish semicircle often found at the base of fingernails. Its presence indicates a healthy person with a strong constitution. The reverse is indicated by the lack of moons: the person may be lacking energy if not physically ill. Some palmists have equated the lack of moons on a man's hands as being an indicator of an inability to commit to a long-term relationship.

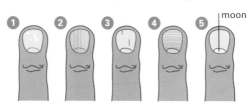

FINGERS AND PHALANGES

The following section looks at each finger in turn, analyzing factors such as individual finger length, width, markings and phalanges. Each finger is associated with a particular planet, each of which has links with classical mythology. Each finger is thought to be revealing of the different areas of a person's character.

The phalanges are the lengths of the fingers between the joints. There are three phalanges on each finger: the basal, middle and initial phalange. Each phalange is associated with a particular astrological symbol and reveals certain personality traits.

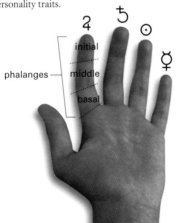

JUPITER
The forefinger, first or index finger In the ancient
Roman pantheon, Jupiter was the chief god and
ruler of the world – the equivalent of the ancient
Greek god Zeus. Appropriately enough the finger
named after this god is associated with the ego,
leadership abilities, ambition and status in the
world.

SATURN
The second, or middle, finger Saturn is considered
the father of Jupiter, and is equivalent to the ancient
Greek god Cromus, who was the god of time. The
Saturn finger is associated with the qualities of
wisdom, sense of responsibility, and general attitude
to life, for example, whether a person is happy or
not.

APOLLO
The third, or ring, finger Apollo, the Sun god and
the god of youth in ancient Roman mythology, was
matched by the Greek god of the same name. In the
same way that the god Apollo is associated with
music and poetry, the Apollo finger reflects a
person's creative abilities and sense of well-being.

MERCURY
The fourth, or little, finger Mercury, from the
Greek god Hermes, is the messenger of the gods.
and this finger is the finger of sexuality
communication; it reveals how articulate a person is
as well as how honest they are in what they say.

ASSESSING PHALANGES

LENGTH

In order to assess the phalanges. the palmist considers such factors as length in comparison to the other phalanges, as well as length in general. In general, the length of a phalange reveals how understanding of and well-versed in the particular area ruled by the phalange that a person is. A lack of length denotes a lack of understanding.

WIDTH

Width is also important. The width of a phalange denotes how experienced and practised in that particular field a person is. The wider the finger, the greater a person utilizes the particular traits ruled by that phalange.

MARKINGS

 Striations are vertical lines. They are generally a good sign since they channel the energy of the phalange, but excessive striations can mean stress.

 Bars are horizontal lines across the phalange that have the opposite effect of striations: they are thought to block the energy expressed by that phalange.

 Grids are cross hatchings of bars and striations that reveal conflict in the realm controlled by that phalange.

2 JUPITER FINGER

Top level with bottom of nail on second finger A leader, a person with the power to govern.

Top below bottom of nail on second finger Timid, feels inferior, avoids responsibility.

Same length as, or longer than, second finger (a) This person is a dictator, self-centred, and one who is determined to make others obey.

Curved in a bow towards second finger Indicates acquisitiveness. This can range from collecting as a hobby if the curve is slight to hoarding and miserliness if the curve is pronounced.

Bending towards second finger This person is persistent and stubborn.

Normal length, but shorter than third finger (b) A good organiser, capable of taking charge, but preferring to work in partnership.

Same length as third finger Well-balanced and self-assured.

Longer than third finger Proud, ambitious, longing for power.

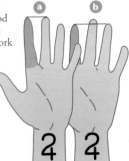

Long and smooth Good prospects in work, business and in the outside world in general.

Short Lacks stamina and confidence.

Very short Self-effacing, frightened of the outside world.

Very thick Dogged and determined.

Very thin A person who will succeed in imagination but not in reality.

Crooked Unscrupulous, determined to get their own way regardless of the consequences.

PHALANGES OF JUPITER
Initial phalange (a)
Associated with Cancer and ruled by the Moon. Revealing of a person's imagination, intuition, goals and spirituality.

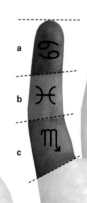

Middle phalange (b)
Associated with Pisces and ruled by Jupiter. Reveals confidence, financial ability and organisational abilities.

Basal phalange (c)
Associated with Scorpio and ruled by Mars. Revealing of a person's status, sexual habitats and relationship with food and drink.

	Phalanges of Jupiter		
	Initial	Middle	Basal
Long	shrewd and has keen insight	organized and has a secure self image	bossy and seeks physical satiation
Short	ambition aimed at material gains	lacks ambition dishonest	not assertive enough
Thin	not in touch with inner mind	doesn't exercise skills enough	laid back, weak, fussy
Wide	successful, and might be rich	used to managing complex tasks	a glutton and a tyrant to work for
Bars	not very shrewd, lacks insight	tends to drop projects and give up	unable to satisfy physical needs
Striations	able to achieve goals	energetic and capable	so-called tired lines that indicate fatigue
Grids	suffers from bad dreams	bottles up emotions	has doubts about self worth

♄ SATURN FINGER

Since the Saturn (middle) finger is often the one used as a baseline to judge the length of others, it can be difficult to assess the length of this finger. Generally, a very long Saturn finger is one that extends a full phalange length above the index and ring fingers. A short Saturn finger is one that is hardly any longer than its neighbours. Overly long or very short Saturn fingers are rare though. So rare, in fact, that some palmists ascribe severe physiological or psychological problems with such a feature.

Straight, and in good proportion to other fingers
A prudent and sensible person, with good concentration and an ability to plan ahead, but who needs privacy.

Long, strong and heavy Serious and thoughtful, likely to have a hard and difficult life.

Same length as first and third fingers (a) Irresponsible, lacks discipline and cannot concentrate for long on any one task. People with such fingers are can be unstable or insecure.

Very long (b) Morbid, melancholic, pedantic, an industrious person but one who is unlikely to be happy.

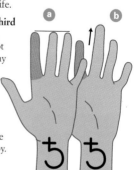

Slightly longer than first and third fingers Dry, cool, socially withdrawn.

Short Intuitive, unintellectual and irresponsible. Has a couldn't care less attitude to life and is severely lacking in any sense of responsibility.

Curved Shows an inclination to the inner or the outer side of life, depending on the direction of the curve.

Crooked Full of self-pity.

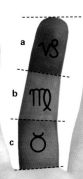

PHALANGES OF SATURN
Initial phalange (a)
Associated with Capricorn and ruled by Saturn. Revealing of a person's intellectual and scientific and logical abilities.

Middle phalange (b)
Associated with Virgo and ruled by Mercury. Revealing of orderliness, ability to plan and think ahead and love of nature.

Basal phalange (c)
Associated with Taurus and ruled by Venus. An Earth phalange associated with earthly things such as material possessions and refinement of tastes.

	Phalanges of Saturn		
	Initial	Middle	Basal
Long	likes to anaylze things serious nature	fond of nature, good detective	good with money
Short	reliable but lacks logical powers	inquiring mind	miserly
Thin	sceptical demands attention	poor organizer	has bad taste
Wide	clear thinker and skilful	very good organizer	has green fingers
Bars	resistant to new ideas	can't concentrate	lacks inner peace
Striations	able to think and respond quickly	fast and efficient at work	has good taste and will invest wisely
Grids	has conflict over what to focus on	unsure about how to plan ahead	can be a sign of sterility in women

⊙ APOLLO FINGER

The normal length of the Apollo finger is considered to be the midway point of the initial phalange of the Saturn (middle) finger.

Strong and smooth Emotionally balanced, creative and perhaps even musical. Artists, entertainers and musicians typically have long Apollo fingers. This is also a sign that the person has a sense of well being.

normal length of Apollo finger is shown by bar

Smooth, with smooth joints The smoother the finger is, the more creative that person is.

Long Conceited, longing for fame, wanting to be in the limelight – a good sign for those with careers in show business or advertising.

Short (a) Shy, lacks emotional control. Short Apollo fingers are also indicative of a lack of creative ability and a low sense of self worth.

Second and third fingers bending together (b) Secretive.

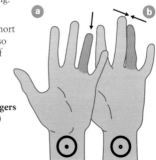

Very long Introverted. The possessor of such a finger is likely to have a gambling instinct, derived from a complete lack of financial inhibition.

Bending towards second finger Anxiety-ridden, defensive.

Bending or drooping towards palm when hand is relaxed Has difficulty in coming to terms with inner or intuitive aspects of the personality.

Crooked or otherwise distorted, or out of proportion to the rest of the hand Emotional difficulties.

Curved towards second finger Afflictions of the heart – these may be emotional or physical.

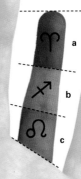

Phalanges of Apollo
Initial phalange (a)
Associated with Aries and ruled by Mars. Revealing of a person's creative inspiration, artistic ideals, desire, courage and anger.

Middle phalange (b)
Associated with Sagittarius and ruled by Jupiter. Reveals artistic pursuits, ability to express one's self, life-style and fitness.

Basal phalange (c)
Associated with Leo and ruled by the Sun. Revealing of a person's artistic skills, vanity, ability to perform creatively and arrogance.

| | **Phalanges of Apollo** | | |
	Initial	Middle	Basal
Long	poetic desires money and luxury	loves art and music	expert musician vain greedy
Short	doesn't like art or music	poor artistic judgment	poor taste
Thin	not concerned with cultural pursuits	poor artistic judgment	insecure about abilities
Wide	passion focused on creative pursuits	expressive leads a busy life	arrogant but able with hands
Bars	creative energy is blocked	cannot express one's self	suffers from 'artist's block'
Striations	bold and inspired	positively uses creative energy	brilliant artist, skilful and inspired
Grids	has problems with keeping temper	may have fitness problems	unable to perform artistically

☿ MERCURY FINGER

The Mercury, or little, finger is considered to be long if it is higher than the middle phalange of the Apollo, or ring, finger. If the finger is low-set, you need to calculate how far up the Apollo finger it would reach if it was not low-set.

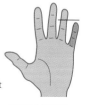

normal length of Mercury finger is shown by bar

Long Highly intelligent, fluent communicator, articulate, expressive and has good business ability. People with long Mercury fingers are knowledgeable and likely to have a considerable interest in education.

Reaching nail on third finger (a) Untrustworthy and may well be a fraudster.

Short (b) Difficulty in making the best of oneself. Finds it hard to put thoughts into words. They probably have a secretive nature and keep themselves to themselves.

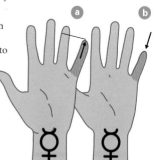

Bending towards third finger Shrewd, clever in business and at making money. Has a tendency to tell white lies.

Bent towards palm when hand is relaxed
Sexual difficulties.

Twisted or crooked Dishonest, a liar, uses questionable business practices.

Sticks out on its own Sexual difficulties.

PHALANGES OF MERCURY
Initial phalange (a)
Associated with Libra and ruled by Venus. Revealing of a person's ideas, metaphysical preoccupations, relationship with culture and sense of humour.

Middle phalange (b)
Associated with Gemini and ruled by Mercury. Reveals how a person translates ideas into action, versatility and ability to listen as well as to deceive.

Basal phalange (c)
Associated with Aquarius and ruled by the Saturn. Revealing of a person's social nature, humanitarian bent, and how they apply their ideals and ideas to everyday life.

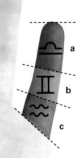

	Phalanges of Mercury		
	Initial	**Middle**	**Basal**
Long	tells tall stories	gift for public speaking	vocation for teaching
Short	lazy mind	not very good with money	degenerate or naive!
Thin	lacks good ideas of own	doesn't like change	likes to play Devil's advocate
Wide	talks too much but is very clever	unscrupulous	sensual and self-indulgent
Bars	cannot be philosophical about life	not much of a talker	lack of imagination
Striations	witty and a good debater	versatile energetic and fit	enjoys sex for its own sake
Grids	unable to express themselves	flighty and a social chameleon	Confused about sexuality

THE THUMB

To many palmists, the thumb is almost as important to a reading as all the fingers put together. This unsurprising really, when you consider that it is the presence of the opposable thumb that is responsible for much of humanity's evolutionary advantages over other mammals. Some Hindu palmists are known to restrict their reading to the thumb alone, and to ignore the rest of the hand!

The thumb bears no god's name (although it is sometimes linked with the first house of the horoscope), but it is a key indicator of the level of vitality or life energy. The larger the thumb, the more vital and powerful the personality, especially when linked with a strong index finger.

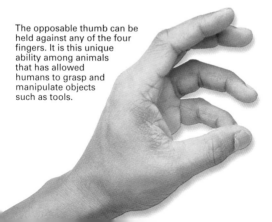

The opposable thumb can be held against any of the four fingers. It is this unique ability among animals that has allowed humans to grasp and manipulate objects such as tools.

LENGTH AND SHAPE OF THE THUMB
When is a thumb considered to be
long? A normal length thumb is level
with the base of the Jupiter (index,
or first) finger. Remember to take
into account the set of the thumb
when assessing length.

Long (a) A good leader, clear-
minded, will-power tempered by
good judgement. People with
long thumbs are very much a ease
with themselves.

a normal-length
thumb

Very long The longer the thumb, the more determined and
forthright a person is. The possessors of very long thumbs
(those that reach the second phalange of the Jupiter finger)
can be tyrannical, despotic and determined to get their
own way at all costs.

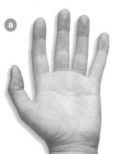

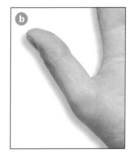

Short Someone with a short thumb is likely to be impressionable and indecisive, one in whom the heart rules the head. The subject may be weak and indecisive, inclined to follow the crowd. These people can lack control of their emotions and are not tactful towards others.

Large Capable and forceful.

Short and thick Obstinate.

Small and weak Lacking in energy and will-power.

Straight (b) Reserved, loyal, reliable, cautious and stubborn.

Smooth joints Full of vitality.

Knotty joints (c) Energy comes in erratic bursts.

Square tip Realistic nature.

Pointed tip (d) Impulsive and impractical.

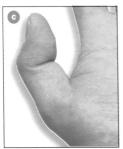
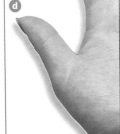

SETTING OF THE THUMB

The point at which the thumb is set into the palm is very revealing. In order to assess what setting a thumb has, divide the palm, or print, into quadrants.

Draw a line from the midpoint of the base of the middle finger (**a**) to the midpoint of the base of the palm (**b**). These points are best judged by eye. If you are looking at an actual hand, the line will be imaginary; if you have a print, however, mark the line on a sheet of tracing paper overlaying the print. The horizontal line of the quadrant division should intersect with the midpoint of the vertical line (**c**). It is best to use a ruler to assess this particular midpoint.

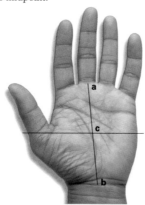

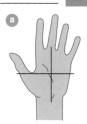

It is important to position the horizontal line of the quadrant division correctly since it determines whether a thumb is set low, high or normally.

Normal-set thumb (a) A normal-set thumb joins the palm at the precise point of intersection between the horizontal quadrant line and the inner edge of the palm. This positioning emphasizes the positive attributes derived from the thumb.

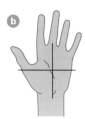

High-set thumb (b) A person with a high-set thumb is likely to be acquisitive, perhaps dishonest and mean; the fact that the thumb will often lie relatively close to the palm reinforces these attributes. These people can be adept problem solvers, however, capable of leaps of creative thinking to come up with unusual solutions.

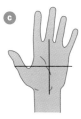

Low set thumb (c) People with low-set thumbs are courageous, versatile and more practically than intellectually gifted. This setting reveals physical vitality, adaptability and generosity.

ANGLE OF THE THUMB

The angle at which a person naturally holds their thumb
out from the palm is linked to their moods, attitudes to
others and level of will-power.

Generally, the wider the angle between the Jupiter (first, or
index) finger and the thumb, the more adventurous and
open towards others a person is. Most people hold their
thumbs out at roughly 45° to 90° from the palm, which
reveals a balanced personality. If the angle is less than 45°,
however, then the person is likely to be selfish and will
probably have a closed mind and keep their will power
cautiously restrained.

Lies close to palm (a) Reflecting the closed nature of such
a hand, these people are rigid and inflexible, with a closed

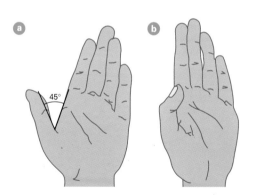

mind. There is also a greater likelihood that the person is not quite honest.

Bent under fingers (b) This hand position reveals someone who is fearful of relationships with others, they keep things hidden and rarely confide their problems. Such a person is likely to be unhappy and self-destructive, perhaps even neurotic.

Forming clear right angle to palm (c) This denotes a strong sense of justice. Such people are relaxed, confident, friendly and open-minded.

Forming an angle greater than a right angle (d) Too tender-hearted and potentially gullible since they are overly trusting of others.

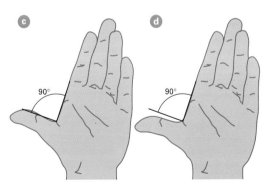

FLEXIBILITY OF THE THUMB

Many novices confuse the angle of the thumb with its
flexibility. Properly, the thumb's flexibility is judged by the
'give' in the top joint . A flexible thumb appears to curve
back on itself slightly, while a stiff thumb is almost
completely straight. The curve will only ever be gentle,
even in a very flexible thumb, however, because this joint
only ever has limited give.

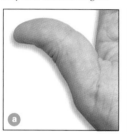
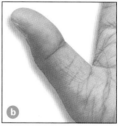

Flexible (a) A flexible nature, easy-going, generous,
tolerant, flexible thumbs appear on people who tend to be
extravagant. These people do not like to fall out with
others or play devil's advocate.

Stiff (b) A sign of determination and resoluteness,
inflexible thumbs are often found on people with
leadership qualities. Such a thumb can be sign of an
unyielding nature, however, almost too firm and too
resolute with a closed mind and showing little sympathy
towards the opinions of others.

PHALANGES OF THE THUMB

As far as the casual observer is concerned, the thumb has only two phalanges. In palmistry, each of these have their own traditional associations – the top phalange is associated with the will, and the middle phalange is associated with logic.

In reality, however, like the fingers, the thumb has three phalanges, but the third is the pad of flesh that frames one side of the palm. This is traditionally put together with the other similarly prominent pads on the hand, which are known as mounts. Therefore, the thumb's third phalange is the Mount of Venus, which is associated with some of the most fundamental aspects of a person's character: their health, vigour, sex drive and general zest for life.

The overall importance of the third phalange in palmistry reflects the fact that it is the joints associated with this phalange that allow the thumb to be opposable.

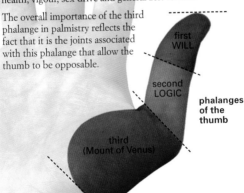

first
WILL

second
LOGIC

**phalanges
of the
thumb**

third
(Mount of Venus)

ANALYSIS OF PHALANGES OF THE THUMB
Drop of water on first phalange

The presence of a drop of water (a little bump that stands out when viewed in profile; see page 64) on the top phalange can be equated with a very acute tactile sense that can literally feel the inherent value or quality of an object. While such drops of water are associated with tactile abilities when present on any of the fingers, one on the thumb is

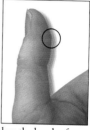

particularly revealing. It is often found on the hands of art connoisseurs or others interested in objects of art.

First and second phalanges are of equal length (a) A well-balanced personality in which will-power and reason are given equal rein. These people are tenacious and able to carry out their plans in a clear and reasoned manner.

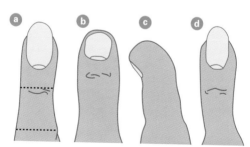

First and second phalanges are of fairly even width (b)
Blunt, outspoken people have such thumbs; they are well used to exercising their logical abilities and getting their own way.

Broad and sturdy first phalange Indicates plenty of stamina and well-directed energy – this is the thumb of a leader. Particularly good if combined with a 'waist' on the second phalange as these people will be able to combine their leadership skills with tact and diplomacy.

First phalange longer than second phalange This person's energy is not controlled by their reasoning powers: they need to 'look before they leap' and more carefully assess situations, listening to the opinions of others before rushing in and trying to do everything their way.

Very tapered first phalange A narrowing of the top phalange indicates a lack of stamina and vitality.

Clubbed first phalange (c) Violent, full of uncontrolled energy. Traditionally, such thumbs have been dubbed 'murderers' thumbs'. In reality, people with such thumbs only have *a tendency* to be violent.

Broad and sturdy second phalange This is the thumb of someone who is logical, thoughtful and who thinks before acting.

Second phalange longer than first phalange Inhibited, feels restricted.

Waisted second phalange (d) Quick-thinking, tactful, impulsive, can be evasive.

4. The Mounts

The fleshy pads on the palm of the hand are called mounts.
They are the landscape onto which the lines are carved,
providing relief and contours that shape the hand. Like the
fingers, they are named after the ancient Roman (and hence
Greek) gods, and like these deities, each has its own sphere
of influence. The base of the thumb, its third phalange, is
called the Mount of Venus. And, like the goddess, or the
planet in astrology, this phalange brings emotional matters to
join will and logic in the thumb's overall range of reference.

As we have already seen, the areas nearer the thumb are
concerned with our relationships with the outside world,
and those farther away with inner matters. So on the other
side of the palm is another important pad of flesh, called the
Mount of the Moon. And it reflects both lunar folklore and
astrological references in its connection with intuitive,
imaginative, even mystic mental activity.

Other mounts around the palm are found at the base of the
fingers. They share the same names as the fingers (the
Mount of Apollo is also known as the Mount of the Sun),
and usually either reinforce or counterbalance what the
fingers reveal. Worthwhile personality clues can also come
from a blurring of the boundaries between the mounts.

Mars, the god of war, does not give his name to any of the
fingers, but instead to two mounts on the hand, the Upper
and Lower mounts of Mars. The upper is linked with moral
courage and resistance; the lower, roughly triangular in
shape, with physical courage and aggression.

1	Mount of Venus	5	Mount of Apollo
2	Lower mount of Mars	6	Mount of Mercury
3	Mount of Jupiter	7	Upper mount of Mars
4	Mount of Saturn	8	Mount of the Moon

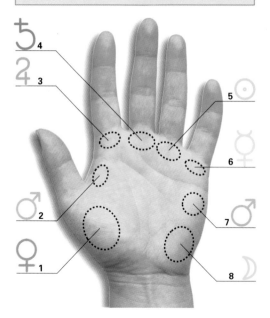

ASSESSING THE MOUNTS

There are various things to consider when evaluating the mounts of a hand, some of which (consistency, for example) cannot be discerned from a hand print but require a physical examination of the actual hand. Until you are familiar with assessing mounts, this task can prove difficult. To better view the mounts of a hand, gently cup your hand, and the mounts will stand out more clearly. When assessing the mounts, it is also important to note what lines of the hand begin and end on each mount and the presence of any particular markings.

DEVELOPMENT OF THE MOUNTS

Perhaps the most important aspect of the mounts is their overall development. Look at their general size and height, comparing them to each other in the process. The mounts on the outer edge of the palm can be used as a baseline. Remember that a lean hand will generally have flatter mounts than a fleshy hand, but development is assessed in comparison to the other mounts on the hand rather than any universal criteria.

The development of a mount reveals how pronounced the qualities it represents are in that person's character. The rule is that the larger the mount is, the more pronounced those qualities will be in that person's character.

There will usually be a dominant mount, which is larger and more developed than the others. The influence of this mount will be greater than that of the others and will 'lead the way' in the analysis of that person's character.

Some mounts may be small, flat or even hollow. The effects of such mounts can range from the energies they channel being expressed negatively to a simple absence of any of the positive attributes associated with that mount.

CONSISTENCY

A firm mount that is springy and elastic to the touch is the perfect consistency since it shows that the mount is channelling its energies positively and actively but not over forcefully. A mount that is flabby to the touch and does not easily regain its shape indicates a weak mount. Hard mounts are a sign of dogmatism and inflexibility.

POSITION

For the digital mounts (those at the base of each finger) positioning can reveal how well the qualities of that mount are accessed. Using a magnifying glass if necessary, find the pinnacle of a mount. If the pinnacle is placed directly under the finger, then the mount is perfectly positioned. If the pinnacle lies between fingers or to one side, then the mount is misplaced, meaning that the person whose hand is being studied may have problems expressing the attributes associated with that mount, or that the effects of that mount will be influenced by neighbouring mounts.

NEGATIVE AND POSITIVE ASSOCIATIONS

Tables on the following pages give the character traits associated with mounts that are positively expressed, that is, mounts that are well developed, neither too small nor too large. Character traits associated with mounts that are negatively expressed are those that are either over-developed, underdeveloped or nonexistent.

♀ MOUNT OF VENUS

Venus, derived from the ancient Greek goddess Aphrodite, was the goddess of love, but this mount's influence goes far beyond romance. In fact, many palmists believe it is the most important mount of all, linking us to our higher selves and acting as a conduit to our will and reasoning powers via the thumb.

It can be difficult to assess the dominance of Venus since it is naturally much larger than other mounts. As a rough guide, a normal sized Mount of Venus takes up about a one-third of the palm's surface.

ASSOCIATIONS

Positive	Negative
• Compassion	• Aggression
• Enthusiasm	• Brutality
• Friendliness	• Ill-health
• Generosity of spirit	• Inhibition
• Health	• Laziness
• Love	• Lewdness
• Luck	• Lecherousness
• Passion	• Restlessness
• Pleasure	• Sexually transmitted
• Sensuality	diseases
• Stamina	• Unfaithfulness
• Vigour	• Unhappiness in love
• Wealth	• Unrefined

VARIATIONS

Broad, firm and rounded Healthy, warm-hearted, sincere, compassionate, loves children.

Flat, underdeveloped Delicate constitution, detached and self-contained nature.

Large A high degree of vitality.

Very large, overdeveloped Extremely energetic physically, hedonistic.

High and firm Highly sexed.

High and soft Excitable and fickle.

Lower part of mount more prominent Energy probably channelled into artistic concerns.

Pale to white in colour Not much concerned with affairs of the heart.

MARKS ON THE MOUNT OF VENUS

 Cross Faithfulness, or a person who has only one great love in his or her life

 Grid Unlucky in love: will encounter many obstacles

 Square Unlikely to suffer from broken romances

MARKS ON THE MOUNT OF VENUS (continued)

 Star If high on mount: lucky in love. If low on mount: family ties will prove more important than romance

 Striations Problematic love life

 Triangle Jealous and manipulative in love

♂ LOWER MOUNT OF MARS

The Lower mount of Mars is named after the Roman god of war (who, in turn, was derived from the Greek war god, Ares). This particular mount of Mars is also referred to as Mars Positive or Mars Active since it reflects the more active, out-going attributes of the war god: strength, courage and aggression. Both mounts are concerned with the person's desire to succeed, will to live, and urge to overcome obstacles. This mount is easier to see if the thumb is held straight next to the palm.

ASSOCIATIONS

Positive	Negative
● Courage	● Anger
● Drive	● Bad tempered
● Energetic	● Belligerent
● Fortitude	● Bullying
● Gallantry	● Competitive
● Keeps a cool head	● Cowardly
● Physical bravery	● Insensitive
● Powerful	● Quarrelsome
● Self-controlled	● Sarcastic
● Stamina	● Violent

VARIATIONS

Normal size Physically brave, resolute, able to keep a cool head in a crisis. A normal sized Lower mount of Mars is a sign of self-control. This is the perfect Lower mount of Mars, its possessors can harness the energy of the mount, but are not hampered by undue temper and aggression.

Large, well-developed Someone with energy and vigour, who tackles life head on. Has a tendency to dislike criticism and feel resentful towards those with more power, though. Can be argumentative.

Very large, overdeveloped Violent and argumentative, possibly cruel and sarcastic, but never afraid of taking risks.

Flat, underdeveloped Cowardly, afraid of physical suffering. This can also be a sign of physical unfitness, and you would be warned to take up some sort of exercise to remedy this.

Absent of hollowed This can reveal very weak characters, unable to assert themselves and afraid of any sort of conflict no matter how mild. They lack the skills to get through day to day obstacles and are prone to depression.

MARKS ON THE LOWER MOUNT OF MARS

Cross Indicates the existence of enemies

Grid A trouble-seeker

Square Often takes risks but rarely suffers consequences

Star Warns against the use of aggression

Striations Can harness anger and put to good use

Triangle Especially courageous

2 MOUNT OF JUPITER

The Mount of Jupiter is named after the king of the gods (Zeus to the ancient Greeks), and like the finger this mount is linked to, it represents authority and sense of self-worth. In astrology, Jupiter is referred to as the 'Greater Fortune' since it stands for pride, position, honour and opportunity.

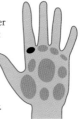

ASSOCIATIONS

Positive	Negative
● Assertive	● Ambition
● Confident	● Arrogant
● Devotion	● Domineering
● Idealism	● Egotism
● Optimism	● Insensitive
● Powerful	● Pride
● Religious	● Overbearing
● Self-controlled	● Selfish
● Self-esteem	● Shrewdness
● Stamina	● Vanity

VARIATIONS

Normal size Enthusiastic, ambitious, good-tempered, friendly. Self-confident and generous. Conventional and conservative at heart, a lover of pomp and ritual.

Wide A generous and friendly person who enjoys the company of others.

Flat, underdeveloped Selfish, lazy, inconsiderate, lacks confidence. People with such mounts of Jupiter are likely to have a poor self-image and feel uncomfortable in large social gatherings.

Very large, overdeveloped Arrogant and overbearing, totally self-centred, driven by ambition.

Connected with the Mount of Saturn Happier working in partnership than alone. Signifies less confidence but greater achievements are possible.

Hollow A natural worrier.

MARKS ON THE MOUNT OF JUPITER

Cross Indicates a love interest that could further career

Grid Bossy and egotistical; selfish and domineering

Square Worldly goods and social position are secure

Star Happiness in love; effortless success

Striations Authoritative and a good leader

Triangle A sign of good luck and success; good organizer

♄ MOUNT OF SATURN

Saturn, named for the ancient god of time, reveals a lot about a person's sense of responsibility, duty, work, business and general disposition.

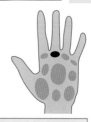

ASSOCIATIONS

Positive	Negative
● Analysis	● Brooding
● Dutiful	● Defensive
● Independent	● Introspective
● Happiness	● Pessimism
● Powerful	● Melancholic
● Prudence	● Self-absorbed
● Responsible	● Selfish
● Self-controlled	● Rigid
● Serious	● Taciturn
● Stamina	● Unhappiness

VARIATIONS

Normal size An introspective nature, serious-minded, studious, prudent. While such people are responsible, they have mastered the happy art of not begrudging duty but rather of learning to enjoy what they have to do.

Flat, underdeveloped A run-of-the-mill person with an unremarkable destiny. Unusually for mounts, it is better for this mount not to be too prominent; its complete absence can denote happiness. Small to flat mounts of Saturn denote people who are kind, serious; dutiful but independent.

Very large, overdeveloped Gloomy, withdrawn, a recluse. Possibly morbid and suicidal.

Positioned towards the Mount of Jupiter A solemn person who aims high.

Positioned towards the Mount of Apollo This person has an intense appreciation of beauty.

MARKS ON THE MOUNT OF SATURN

Cross Warning to remember responsibilities

Grid Depression likely; morbid and introspective

Square Will not suffer from financial worries

Star Can indicate or warn of a sudden end

Striations Authoritative and a good leader

Triangle An interest in science or the occult

MOUNT OF APOLLO (MOUNT OF THE SUN)

Like the finger it is linked to and the Roman god it is named after (the god of youth represented by the Sun and patron of the arts and poetry), the mount of Apollo is revealing of a person's creative abilities and emotions. Generally, the larger the mount the more pronounced are the drives for fame and fortune.

ASSOCIATIONS

Positive	Negative
● Brilliant	● Conceited
● Creative	● Disinterest in wider world
● Enthusiastic	
● Expansive	● Extravagant
● Glory	● Lack of imagination
● Lively	● Ostentatious
● Optimistic	● Pretentious
● Talented	● Proud
● Self-publicist	
● Successful	

VARIATIONS

Normal size A pleasant, sunny nature, with a lucky streak. Has good taste and artistic leanings. The presence of such a mount reveals a fortunate person.

Flat, underdeveloped Leads a dull, aimless existence, and has no interest in the arts or any form of culture. They may well make up for these deficiencies, however, with a well-developed practical streak.

Very large, overdeveloped Pretentious, extravagant and hedonistic. Of all the mounts, however, this is the least problematic one to have as a dominant mount. Possessors are greatly interested in music and the arts, and have a great love of pleasure.

Positioned towards the mount of Mercury Able to make money from the arts. If it actually connects with the Mount of Mercury, then any introvert or extrovert tendencies shown in the fingers will be reinforced.

MARKS ON THE MOUNT OF APOLLO

✕   **Cross** Hopes may come to naught

▦   **Grid** Will be infamous rather than famous

▢   **Square** Reputation is unbesmirchable

✳   **Star** Wealth, prestige and success in artistic field

   Striations Creative energies are effectively channelled

   Triangle Will achieve long-term success

☿ MOUNT OF MERCURY

Communications is the realm ruled by both the mount and finger of Mercury. Mercury, or Hermes to the ancient Greeks, was also the god of science, medicine, learning and philosophy. Communication and the ability to relate to others is at the heart of the civilizing power of thought, leading to endeavour in these scientific fields.

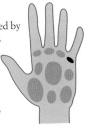

ASSOCIATIONS

Positive	Negative
● Eloquent	● Boastful
● Intellectual	● Dishonest
● Inventive	● Garrulousness
● Imaginative	● Irritable
● Logical	● Lack of financial acumen
● Reasonable	● Nervous
● Scientific	● Sensitive
● Studious	● Socially inept

VARIATIONS

Normal size Quick-thinking but subtle. Lively, persuasive, hard-working, needs variety and company.

Flat, underdeveloped Dull, gullible, and humourless.

Large A good sense of humour.

Very large, overdeveloped A sharp conman, materialistic and light-fingered, a cheat.

MARKS ON THE MOUNT OF MERCURY

 Cross Gullible and foolish; warns against cheats

 Grid Cunning and dishonest

 Square Protects against stress and mental strain

 Star Success in academia

 Striations So-called 'medical stigmata', signifying caring and compassionate nature; found on hands of doctors and nurses

 Triangle Influential communicator; success in business

♂ UPPER MOUNT OF MARS

Like the Lower mount of Mars, the Upper mount of Mars is also linked to the god of war but it expresses the more passive, or negative, aspects of the deity. For this reason this mount is sometimes called Mars Passive or Mars Negative. It is linked with the traits of

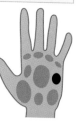

endurance, self-control and while still representative of fighting abilities, they are covertly expressed.

ASSOCIATIONS

Positive	Negative
● Moral courage	● Vengeful
● Resistance	● Violent
● Endurance	● Lustful
● Excitability	● Obscene
● Desire	● Jealousness
● Sexuality	● Crafty

VARIATIONS

Normal size Morally courageous. Someone with such a mount of Mars will seem to be difficult to annoy, calm and self-controlled but in fact they just have a very long fuse. So watch out, they can only be pushed so far.

Flat, underdeveloped Cowardly, interested only in self-preservation, has no staying power and is likely to have no charisma.

Very large, overdeveloped Bad-tempered, sarcastic, mentally cruel. These people are so persistent that they will keep going even when they should give up, 'literally' flogging a dead horse. They are very good, however, at coping under great pressure.

MARKS ON THE UPPER MOUNT OF MARS

 Cross Reveals secret enemies or physical injury

 Grid Can't control temper

 Square Has great endurance

 Star Stubborn and quarrelsome

 Striations Has the courage of convictions

Triangle Campaigns against injustice: fights for the underdog

MOUNT OF THE MOON

Just as the moon has taken on feminine characteristics in popular mythology, so has the mount named after it. This mount is the focus of the inner, hidden world as represented by its half of the palm. Therefore, the Mount of the Moon represents the hidden, inner side of our emotional lives and unconscious drives. Though it can veer towards the passive it always signifies great receptivity and nurturing qualities when present in men or women. The nearer the mount appears to the wrist, the more exaggerated are the intuitive and creative abilities.

ASSOCIATIONS

Positive	Negative
● Receptive	● Delirious
● Sensitive	● Madness
● Intuitive	● Sadness
● Imaginative	● Hysteria
● Dreamy	● Over imaginative
● Visionary	● Lack of objectivity
● Psychic	
● Affectionate	
● Maternal	

VARIATIONS

Normal size Sensitive and perceptive, romantic and imaginative, artistic, possibly with a great love of the sea. Family and travel for the purposes of broadening the mind are close to these people's hearts.

Flat, underdeveloped (a) Unimaginative, unsympathetic, unstable, cold, bigoted.

Very large, overdeveloped Over-imaginative, introspective, probably untruthful and perhaps also hysterical.

High and firm Creative, with a powerful and fertile imagination. If it is also near to the wrist, then expect paranormal abilities.

High and soft Touchy, thin-skinned, fickle dreamers who like the sound of their own voices.

Reaching to the Mount of Venus Extremely passionate.

MARKS ON THE MOUNT OF THE MOON

 Cross Tells tall tales; leaps before looking

 Grid Suffers from stress

Square WIll make long, obstacle-strewn journeys

Star Takes risks; cannot keep secrets

Striations Possesses psychic or intuitive abilities

 Triangle Artistic and literary success

MOUNT OF NEPTUNE

As well as the main mounts discussed here, there is a rarely seen mount named after the Roman god of the sea, Neptune. When present, this mount is located at the centre of the palmar base between the Mount of the Moon and the Mount of Venus, thus straddling the subconscious and conscious sides of the palm and reflecting the reserve of human instinctual knowledge.

As a result of its position, this mount indicates someone who is attuned to nature and natural remedies, they make excellent healers or practitioners of complementary therapies since they can utilize and channel their subconscious knowledge. Such people tend also to be leaders, but they are more likely to be the charismatic leader of a political or religious movement than a more conventional business or military leader.

PLAIN OF MARS

In the middle of palm, and delineated by the surrounding mounts, lies the plain of Mars. If this area is hollow, then the owner of that hand will lack presence, but if the plain is fleshy and well-padded and firm to the touch, then a potentially violent temper is revealed. This is because the plain of Mars reveals the energy levels of a person.

COMPATIBILITY AND THE MOUNTS

Assessing and comparing the development of two people's
mounts can reveal truths about how well the couple are
likely to get on. Each of the following tables compares a
particular mount.

MOUNT OF VENUS

♀	Under-developed	Well-developed	Over-developed
Under-developed	Relationship may lack fire as both are inhibited and lack passion.	The imbalance in ability to express passion may prove to be a problem.	The two are interested and inspired by different things.
Well-developed	The well-developed one should try to understand the other's reserve.	Both share the same balanced approach to life so they could get on very well.	Potentially a good match as they share a similar approach to life.
Over-developed	An unhappy match as one will overwhelm the other.	Another good match as both like to enjoy a vigorous sex life.	These two may burn each other out with their demands.

LOWER MOUNT OF MARS

♂	Under-developed	Well-developed	Over-developed
Under-developed	Though these two are very similar, they are almost too meek to get on with each other.	The confidence and drive of the one with the larger mount could make up for the other's lack of stamina and energy.	An unfortunate match for the one with the smaller mount as they might be bullied and pushed around by the other.
Well-developed	Though it could work, the one with the smaller mount may not be able to keep up with the other.	A perfect match: both are assertive, confident and optimistic. These two could be very happy together.	It is fine line between this relationship working and failing. They need to tolerate each other's differences.
Over-developed	The only way this match could work is if the dominant partner takes a protective role towards the other.	The one with the larger mount will want to be the leader, and this will cause the two to clash.	These two will either get on famously, acting as trouble makers together, or they will hate each other.

MOUNT OF JUPITER

2

	Under-developed	Well-developed	Over-developed
Under-developed	Together, these two might be able to find refuge from society, where they generally do not fit in.	The partner with the larger mount may be able to boost the other's poor self-image enough to make this match work.	An unhealthy match: one partner is overbearing, and the other lacks the will to stand up to bad treatment.
Well-developed	These two may find that one wants to go out socializing while the other prefers to stay in and chat.	A happy match: neither will challenge the other's sense of self-worth; in fact, each will boost the other's ego.	If the partner with the smaller mount is assertive enough, this match could work out.
Over-developed	An unlikely match: the one with the larger mount may not be interested unless the other can offer some advantage.	The partner with the larger mount may put the other off with their self-seeking ambition.	Two potentially violent and generally argumentative people make for a stormy relationship.

MOUNT OF SATURN

	Under-developed	Well-developed	Over-developed
Under-developed	These two are both kind and serious: they are likely to have a fulfilling and secure relationship together.	These two are very similar and likely to get on well. Both are easy-going enough to smooth over any rucks.	Hopefully, the one with the smaller mount will be understanding and able to put up with the other's gloominess.
Well-developed	A long though not always exciting relationship will be possible, unless one of them has a hollow mount.	These two will stick together through thick and thin; it may be their sense of loyalty, or duty, that keeps them united.	The one with the smaller mount may be philosophical enough to love the other despite their oddities.
Over-developed	Discussing their feelings will be a problem: one is withdrawn, so the other will need excellent communication skills.	It is likely that these two can get on, but both are very serious-minded, so they might not have much fun!	Both are naturally reclusive, so there is only hope if they enjoy each other's company a great deal.

MOUNT OF APOLLO

	Under-developed	Well-developed	Over-developed
Under-developed	These two might get on if either of them can ever make the first move.	The things that make one tick just turn the other off; it is hard to see how these two can enjoy each other's company.	The one with the larger mount is far too extravagant to appeal to the other; these two are unlikely to fall in love.
Well-developed	The one with the larger mount will need to have a practical streak to make this relationship work.	Such a pair are likely to share a happy, easy-going relationship blessed by good fortune.	These two can be very happy: together both are passionate, though the one with the larger mount more so than the other.
Over-developed	Not a good match: one has a low sex drive (the one with the smaller mount), and the other has a very high sex drive.	The only fly in the ointment may be the owner of the larger mount's inability to apologize for any misdeeds.	A passionate couple prone to public displays of affection; they will enjoy a riotous 'nightlife' together.

MOUNT OF MERCURY

☿	Under-developed	Well-developed	Over-developed
Under-developed	Both of these find it difficult to talk openly about their feelings, the pair need to suffer few problems to last.	The one with the larger mount may be persuasive enough to bring the other out of their shell.	If the size difference is large, the one with the smaller mount should take care not to be too trusting.
Well-developed	It would help the match if the one with the smaller mount made an effort to be more open and talkative.	These two revel in each other's company, and they are able to talk openly about all aspects of their relationship.	These two can be a good match if they can keep their sense of humour and keep talking to each other.
Over-developed	If the size difference is not too great, then it can be hoped each will be able to improve the other's faults.	The one with the larger mount tends to annoy the other with their garrulousness.	Any kind of relationship between these two will be productive, whether a romance or a business venture.

UPPER MOUNT OF MARS

♂	Under-developed	Well-developed	Over-developed
Under-developed	Both partners probably need someone more pushy to give this relationship any hope.	This can be a good match for the one with the smaller mount, as they will be encouraged to assert themselves.	The partner with the smaller mount is likely to be the doormat in this relationship.
Well-developed	One has a very short temper (or panic threshold) while the other can be quite patient, but only up to a certain point.	Once the basic ground rules are established (and kept to!), this couple can be very content, even exciting to each other.	Arguments can be frequent and bitter, but they just might be able to thrash out their differences in this way.
Over-developed	This is only possible if the one with larger mount has an urge to protect the meek, nonetheless they will feel stifled.	The one with the smaller mount will run out of patience with the other's bad temper.	Each will be busy punishing the other for imagined slights; it is hoped they will have the sense to separate.

MOUNT OF THE MOON

	Under-developed	Well-developed	Over-developed
Under-developed	Typically a cold and loveless union.	The one with the smaller mount will dash the hopes of their partner of a mutually supportive relationship.	This could work since the one with the smaller mount may simply fail to notice the other's bad moods.
Well-developed	The one with the larger mount needs to assess the relationship carefully and not rely on their intuition.	Soulmates: these two are made for each other, and they are likely to have a very long and happy relationship.	The partner with the smaller mount will be lucky in love if they can balance their partner's wilder tendencies.
Over-developed	One partner may find themselves being mothered too much by the other, which may not be a bad thing.	If the size difference isn't too great these two are destined for a passionate romance.	These two are both dark horses, who may well harbour deeper feelings for each other than they are able to show.

HEALTH AND THE MOUNTS

The development of mounts can indicate the likelihood of certain problems arising. Always look for other signs on the hand, however, and never diagnose health matters unless you are very confident in your abilities.

	Under-developed	Well-developed	Over-developed
Mount of Venus	doesn't take enough exercise has a delicate constitution lacks stamina	has a generally healthy constitution has plenty of stamina	should take particular care not to practice unsafe sex has loads of energy
Lower mount of Mars	has a tendency toward hypochondria has little resistance to disease	is prone to skin complaints has plenty of stamina	is prone to high blood pressure has a strong immune system
Mount of Jupiter	prone to worry and depression lacks energy	has plenty of stamina and energy easily recovers from most illnesses	self-indulgent tendencies could lead to obesity is prone to heartburn

	Under-developed	Well-developed	Over-developed
Mount of Saturn	has poor circulation legs, teeth or ears may be problematic	is likely to live a long life may suffer from rheumatism	is prone to depression, or even manic depression
Mount of Apollo	is prone to throat problems and blood disorders	has very good health and is rarely ill but needs to take care of heart	should take particular care not to practice unsafe sex
Mount of Mercury	nervous problems may have diction problems	has a healthy mental constitution may have fragile bones	prone to liver disease and indigestion
Upper mount of Mars	has a weak immune system is prone to allergies	has a strong immune system may be prone to bruising	has a strong mental constitution and not prone to stress
Mount of Moon	may have a history of mental problems	may have ability to heal is prone to lymphatic disorders	prone to panic attack nervous problems are likely

CAREER AND THE MOUNTS

Assessing the relative development of a person's mounts can help evaluate what someone's strengths and weaknesses in the work environment are. Then you can predict likely occupations, or advise on suitable jobs.

ABILITIES AND WEAKNESSES

	Under-developed	Well-developed	Over-developed
Mount of Venus	has little enthusiasm for their work does not like to travel	is an all-round good worker able to reason logically is a good communicator	is charismatic, but not a good leader irresponsible at work very logical
Lower mount of Mars	amenable (largely due to their fear of open conflict)	has great integrity can keep a cool head keen to develop skills	a good manipulator an aggressive opponent treads on others toes
Mount of Jupiter	prefers to work alone	has good leadership skills has a keen sense of justice	is very generous is a tireless self-promoter financially astute

	Under-developed	Well-developed	Over-developed
Mount of Saturn	lacks motivation is not a good time-keeper	is highly motivated and conscientious about work studious	takes work very seriously but doesn't particularly enjoy it
Mount of Apollo	probably has a practical streak lacks ambition	has good artistic taste has creative abilities enjoys fashion	has great artistic and creative flair can be temperamental
Mount of Mercury	has poor communication skills lacks motivation	an able communicator is intelligent can think laterally	able to inspire and motivate others can be precocious
Upper mount of Mars	hates conflict, so can be an effective team worker underhand	able to lead and work with others only assertive when needed	can be too bossy: watch out for harassment accusations!
Mount of Moon	has little sympathy for others lacks imagination	imaginative and intuitive organized logical	likes to travel can be unreliable

SUITABLE OCCUPATIONS

	Under-developed	Well-developed	Over-developed
Mount of Venus	freelance worker, or anything at which they can be self-employed	anything in one of the caring professions, especially if with children	anything physically demanding entertainer artist actor
Lower mount of Mars	librarian something that involves teamwork but not taking the lead	coroner judge or magistrate politician surgeon paramedic	athlete stock broker financial analyst insurance salesperson
Mount of Jupiter	delivery person (post, milk, or other goods) cab driver traveller	banker farmer civil servant member of the clergy	charity worker or volunteer fundraiser music promoter
Mount of Saturn	freelance worker, but unlikely to run own company	scientist researcher academic news reader architect	accountant banker policy maker civil servant manager copy-editor

	Under-developed	**Well-developed**	**Over-developed**
Mount of Apollo	farmer builder cycle courier cab driver computer operator	artist sculptor actor dancer critic model	salesperson poet playwright choreographer opera singer designer
Mount of Mercury	clerical worker librarian bus driver telephone operator	anything in the media teacher politician scientist philosopher	advertising executive a manager in any media business architect
Upper mount of Mars	nightclub bouncer police officer security guard mediator	soldier sports coach farmer builder in public relations	football manager army officer athlete accountant actor
Mount of the Moon	police officer traffic warden tax collector bailiff	member of the clergy sailor philosopher painter sculptor	artist actor spiritualist computer programmer inventor

5. Lines on the Hand

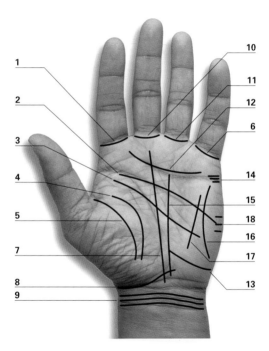

1 Solomon's ring	**10** Ring of Saturn
2 Heartline	**11** Ring of Apollo
3 Headline	**12** Girdle of Venus
4 Lifeline	**13** Child lines
5 Line of Mars	**14** Lines of marriage
6 Family ring	**15** Line of the Sun
7 Line of Fate	**16** Line of intuition
8 Via Lasciva	**17** Hepatica
9 Rascettes, or bracelets	**18** Travel lines

The three major lines – the head, heart and life lines – appear on nearly every hand. Although it is possible to have one or more of these lines missing, in practice it is unlikely that you will ever see such a palm.

The lifeline does not indicate how long you will live: the old wives' tale that a short lifeline indicates a short life should be forgotten. What the lifeline does show is the strength of a person's vitality, their 'life energy', and so it should be read in conjunction with the thumb, the finger of Jupiter and the mount of Venus, which are also important in this area. Similarly, the heartline, which is concerned with our emotions and sexuality should be referred to those other indicators of our feelings, the finger of Mercury and the mount of Venus.

The headline is concerned with our mental attitudes. Like all the lines in the palm, it should be related to the shape of the hand. For example, you would normally expect to find a straight headline on a practical hand; a sloping headline would be unusual (though it could indicate a person who uses their imagination in a practical way, perhaps a designer or inventor). But a sloping headline on a sensitive hand would merely act as a confirmation of the imaginative nature you had already suspected.

Unlike the major lines, the minor lines – the line of fate, the line of the Sun, and so on – can be present or absent. Indeed, the lines on the palm can and do change, growing clearer or less clear, developing disruptions or losing them. So it would not be surprising to see a strong line of fate (the most changeable of all the lines) in the hand of an adult where there had not been one in the child. And in some cases, we would certainly prefer the line to be absent: the more robust your constitution, the less likely you are to have the misnamed line of health, or Hepatica, in your hand.

Of the more commonly occurring lines, the line of fate relates to our destiny; the line of the Sun to our good fortune, creativity and satisfaction; the girdle of Venus to passion; the Via Lasciva to our desires – for money, sensual pleasure and so on; and the bracelets to health, wealth and travel. The lines of health, marriage, children and influence have their own eponymous spheres of influence.

The presence of a variety of marks on each line also needs to be considered. Each mark has a general meaning, given in the following table; more specific readings relating to the appearance of each mark on a particular line are given in the sections on devoted to particular lines.

LINE FORMATIONS AND MARKINGS

The appearance of lines can vary greatly. They may be incisive and clear, or interrupted and embellished by a series of secondary lines or marks. The presence of such features on the major and minor lines of the hand affects the reading of each line.

Mark	Formation/General meaning
Bar	
	Small line cutting across palmar line opposition to energy of line, perhaps linked to a generally brief period of stress or trauma
Branch	
	ascending emphasizes power and strength of main line
	descending negates power and strength of main line
Break	
	clean failure: absence of function in realm ruled by the broken line: the energy of line has been broken
	overlapping doubling of energy flowing through the line

Mark	Formation/General meaning
Chain	
	a series of islands denotes weakness or reveals a period of conflict
Cross	
	similar to bar but with extra focusing of negative energy at point of intersection, revealing particularly bad experiences
Forked end	
	even branches a positive splitting of energy, favourably shared between two branches
	uneven branches a negative splitting signifying a dispersal of energy
Grid	
	indicates conflict and indecision as well as inability to act
Island	
	obstructs correct functioning of ability / realm denoted by line as it weakens the line; indicates low resistance to ill events

Mark	Formation/General meaning
Sister line	
	a fine line running alongside a major line the main line is 'bridged over' by this line, lessening any negative denotations carried by the main line
Spots	an intense focusing of positive energy but a series of spots can reveal marked disparities in a person's ability to perform over a sustained period of time
Square	protects against misfortune in realm dealt with by line
Star	similar to bar and cross but with even more intense focusing of, generally negative, energy at point of intersection, revealing really bad experiences. This intensification can sometimes lead to positive experiences though
Striation	**faint vertical lines replacing main line** indicates a dispersal of energy, a mental or physical block that may not be constant; effects of striation can lead to haphazard functioning of line's abilities

Mark	Formation/General meaning
Tasselled end	
	indicates weakness and dissipation of energies
Triangle	
	Along with the square, the triangle is one of the few marks to be found on the hand with positive associations. Its presence reveals the concentration of intellectual ability and brain power.

HEADLINE

Length This indicates the level of intelligence, breadth of understanding and use made of intellectual potential. The longer the line, the greater the importance played by intellectual matters.

Straight across palm (1) Practical and realistic, down-to-earth, a good organizer.

Long and straight Shrewd, a good forward planner with a good memory.

Sloping towards Mount of the Moon (2) Sensitive and imaginative.

Long, reaching top part of Mount of the Moon (3) A talent for self-expression.

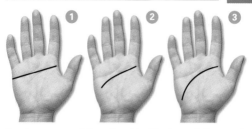

Curving up towards heartline Good business ability, good at making money.

Starts just touching lifeline (4) A prudent, moderate and balanced nature.

Starts with a small separation from lifeline (5) Long, reaching lower part of Mount of the Moon Over-imaginative. Independent and enterprising, in need of a definite direction in life to prevent wasting energy on trivia.

Starts with a wide separation from lifeline (6) Foolhardy and excitable.

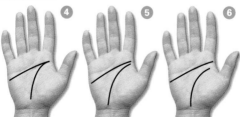

Running close to heartline Narrow in outlook.

Weak and some distance from lifeline This person has a tendency to gamble.

Clear and distinct Good concentration.

Running towards centre of wrist Out of touch with reality.

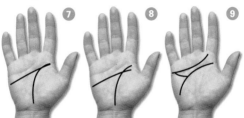

Starts linked to lifeline for some distance (7) Very cautious. Needs encouragement and responds badly to criticism.

Starts inside lifeline on Mount of Mars (8) Touchy, irritable.

Ends with a large fork that touches both Mount of the Moon and the heartline (9) Able to be subsumed in another's personality, will give up everything for love.

Long, sloping ends with an even fork Clever and diplomatic, with a talent for self-expression.

Straight, ends with a small fork pointing to the Mount of the Moon (10) Imagination restrained by common sense.

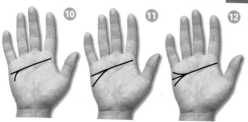

Ends in a large fork (11) Too versatile, unable to achieve excellence in any one thing.

Ends in a three-pronged fork (12) Combines intelligence, imagination and business ability.

Branchline to Mount of Jupiter (13) Ambitious and successful.

Branchline to Mount of Saturn (14) Ambitious, but will have to struggle for success.

Branchline to Mount of Apollo (15) Achieving success through the use of own talents.

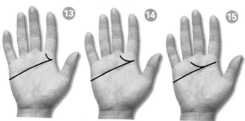

Ends in Mount of Mercury Very good at making money – has the Midas touch.

Branchline ending between third and fourth fingers A successful scientist or inventor.

Branchline to Mount of Mercury Successful in business.

TIMING EVENTS ON THE HEADLINE

An important aspect of palmistry involves calculating when particular events occurred.

a) The 20-year mark falls directly below the inside edge of the index, or Jupiter, finger.

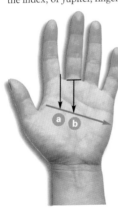

b) The 35-year mark falls directly below the midpoint of the base of the Saturn (middle) finger.

Using these two points as a guide, you can divide the line up into equally spaced 15 year periods, and even further subdivide those sections if you wish.

If you know when a particular event occurred in someone's life, and you can see this event reflected in their palm, then you can use this information to check the accuracy of your time gauge on the line.

MARKS ON THE HEADLINE

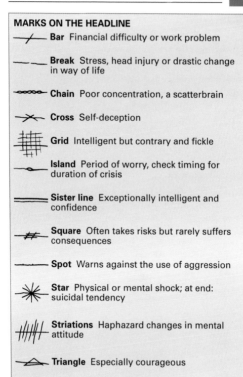

Bar Financial difficulty or work problem

Break Stress, head injury or drastic change in way of life

Chain Poor concentration, a scatterbrain

Cross Self-deception

Grid Intelligent but contrary and fickle

Island Period of worry, check timing for duration of crisis

Sister line Exceptionally intelligent and confidence

Square Often takes risks but rarely suffers consequences

Spot Warns against the use of aggression

Star Physical or mental shock; at end: suicidal tendency

Striations Haphazard changes in mental attitude

Triangle Especially courageous

HEARTLINE

Long, generously curved and some distance from the bases of the fingers Warm-hearted, sensual, demonstrative.

Longer and stronger than headline The heart rules the head.

Straight Reserved and self-interested.

Short and faint A limited capacity for love.

Very long, deep and close to the fingers Possessive, jealous.

Blurred appearance Tendency to emotional difficulties.

Many small branches (1) A vivid, dynamic personality. Each branch represents a romantic attachment, pointing upward for those that are successful and downward for those that are not.

Broken in several places Unfaithful, lacks constancy.

Starts in middle of Mount of Jupiter (2) Fussy and discriminating when choosing friends and lovers, extremely loyal to those chosen. Seeks to marry well.

Starts with a fork on Mount of Jupiter (3) Lovable and easy to live with, makes a good marriage partner.

Starts with a large fork, one prong on Mount of Jupiter and one on Mount of Saturn (4) Changeable, moody, has difficulty in living with others.

Starts between fingers of Saturn and Jupiter A relationship that involves friendship as well as love.

Starts on Mount of Saturn (5) Sensual, but lacking real depth of feeling for others.

Branchline running to headline (6) A partner met through work, or a marriage that is a working partnership.

Chainlike appearance and starting on Mount of Saturn
Contempt for the opposite sex.

Starts at same point as headline and lifeline Extremely
selfish and lacks any control over the emotions.

Running together with headline as one line Known as the
'simian line'. A sign of enormous internal struggle, possibly
of mental handicap.

Branchline running to fateline A romance, if the
branchline does not touch the fateline; a wedding if they
just touch; an unhappy marriage if they cross.

TIMING EVENTS ON THE HEARTLINE
There is great debate over whether or not it is possible to
time events on the heartline, and even disagreement as to
which way across the palm the heartline should be read.

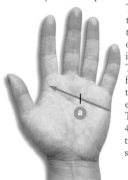

The consensus seems to be
that the heartline runs from
the percussion (outside edge
of the palm) towards the
index, or Jupiter, finger.
To time events on this line,
find the midpoint (by eye, as
the method is not exact
enough to warrant a ruler).
This point will be roughly the
40-year mark (**a**), then divide
the line into equal 5-year
sections accordingly.

MARKS ON THE HEARTLINE

Bar Outside interference in love life is likely

Break Jilted, or emotional trauma leading to emotional blockage; overlapping break: a reconciliation

Chain A flirt and emotionally unstable

Cross A bad love affair or emotionally traumatic experience

Grid Unable to commit to a long-term relationship

Island Guilt and emotional distress expected; refer to nearest mount for realm affected

Sister line Leads a double emotional life; perhaps a bigamist?

Square Will get over heartbreaks

Spot Emotionally focused and passionate

Star Predicts happiness in love and good fortune

Striations Inconstancy, flirtatious, has many short-lived affairs

Triangle Able to think clearly about emotional matters

LIFELINE

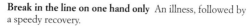

Long and clear Good vitality, a healthy constitution.

Short and chequered Lacks energy, may be physically frail.

Discontinuities in the line Changes in direction of life.

Break in the line on one hand only An illness, followed by a speedy recovery.

Break in the line on both hands A more serious illness with a more troublesome and problematic recovery.

Many small branches running upward Good health, prosperity.

Many small branches running downward Poor health, financial setbacks.

Starts on mount of Jupiter (1) Highly ambitious – and likely to succeed.

Starts from headline (2) Very controlled and calculating.

Starts well below headline (3) Lacks control, uninhibited.

Ends in a fork with one branch ending in mount of the moon Indicates long-distance travel.

Two small branches from beginning of line onto headline (4) An inheritance: could be money, but more likely to have been given a good start in life by parents.

Branchline to headline from halfway down line (5) Success and recognition will come in middle age.

Branchline to Mount of Saturn Life will be a struggle, must make own way without outside help.

Branchline to Mount of the Sun (6) Talents will be recognized and rewarded.

Branchline to Mount of Jupiter Self-confident and self-assured.

Branchline to Mount of the Moon A longing for a new stimulus, for change. Traditionally, a sea journey.

TIMING EVENTS ON THE LIFELINE

On a handprint, draw a line from the inside of the Jupiter, or index, finger, straight down to the lifeline. The point at which the two lines intersect is the 20-year mark (**a**). Using this as a guide, mark 20-, 10 and 5-year intervals along the remainder of the lifeline.

Timing short lifelines On closer inspection of 'short' lifelines you will see that towards the end of the lifeline, a branch will connect it to another line, the fate line for example; this line then completes the curve of the lifeline. This reflects a major change in the person's life, such as moving to a foreign country.

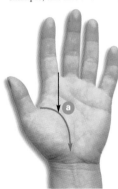

Timing broken, overlapping lifelines If the lines overlap, transfer the timeline to the new section where the two overlap. This formation also denotes a major lifestyle change.

MARKS ON THE LIFELINE

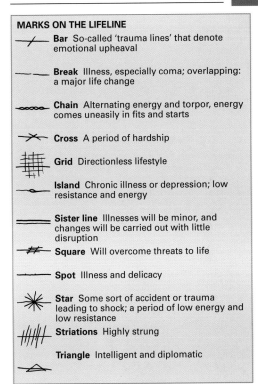

Bar So-called 'trauma lines' that denote emotional upheaval

Break Illness, especially coma; overlapping: a major life change

Chain Alternating energy and torpor, energy comes uneasily in fits and starts

Cross A period of hardship

Grid Directionless lifestyle

Island Chronic illness or depression; low resistance and energy

Sister line Illnesses will be minor, and changes will be carried out with little disruption

Square Will overcome threats to life

Spot Illness and delicacy

Star Some sort of accident or trauma leading to shock; a period of low energy and low resistance

Striations Highly strung

Triangle Intelligent and diplomatic

LINE OF FATE

No line A smooth and uneventful life.

Weak or faint line A directionless and unsettled life.

Straight and unbroken A successful, untroubled life. A self-motivated and strong individual with leadership abilities.

Wavy Argumentative, changeable, disorganised.

Reaching Mount of Saturn Trying to exceed own powers.

Curved towards Mount of Jupiter Success through effort.

Starts from headline or heartline Success late in life.

Starts from lifeline (1) Hampered by early environment and family surroundings. Point of separation of lines shows when independence was or will be achieved.

Starts from top bracelet (2) Early responsibility.

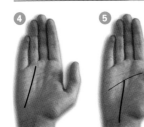

Starts from Mount of Venus, ends on Mount of Saturn (3)
A secure and loved childhood, supported by parents and
family. Possibly success through inheritance.

Starts from Mount of the Moon (4) A varied life, much
travelling will be involved.

Ends on headline Prone to errors of judgement, bad
planning that leads to misfortune.

Ends on heartline (5) Sacrifices necessary in the cause of
love or duty.

Ends on Mount of the Sun Popular and talented.
Branchline to line of the sun A successful partnership. If
the lines cross, the partnership will fail.

Branchline to Mount of Mercury (6) Achievement and
wealth obtained through business or science.

Branchline to Mount of Apollo Denotes fame or fortune,
or both.

TIMING EVENTS ON THE LINE OF FATE

On a handprint, draw a line from the base of the Saturn, or middle, finger straight down to the first rascette, or bracelet, on the wrist. The midpoint of this line is the 40-year mark (**a**). Using this as a guide to divide up the rest of the line, mark 20-year, 10-year and 5-year intervals along the remainder of the vertical line. Transfer the markings on the timeline straight across to the fateline to time events.

MARKS ON THE LINE OF FATE

Bar Theft, burglary or robbery; money lost

Break Sudden change in circumstances; overlapping: planned changes

Chain Period of unhappiness, insecurity and unforeseen difficulties

Cross Threat to career, loss of material wealth; warns against recklessness if on Mount of Saturn

Grid A hapless timewaster and ne'er do well

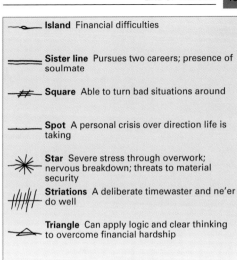

Island Financial difficulties

Sister line Pursues two careers; presence of soulmate

Square Able to turn bad situations around

Spot A personal crisis over direction life is taking

Star Severe stress through overwork; nervous breakdown; threats to material security

Striations A deliberate timewaster and ne'er do well

Triangle Can apply logic and clear thinking to overcome financial hardship

LINE OF THE SUN (OR LINE OF APOLLO, OR LINE OF FORTUNE)

No line A life of disappointments and setbacks, however talented the owner of the hand.

Clear and straight A lucky person with a charming and sunny nature.

Blurred Lacks concentration, wastes effort.

Starts close to wrist between Mounts of Venus and the Moon, ends in Mount of the Sun (1) Nothing ever goes wrong in this life.

Starts from lifeline or line of fate, ends on Mount of Sun Success as a result of using talents and energy.

Starts from headline (2) Success in middle age as result of own efforts.

Starts from heartline (3) Warmth, happiness and sufficiency in old age.

Starts from Mount of Venus (4) Artistically gifted.

Starts from Mount of the Moon (5) Strongly attractive to the opposite sex, a person idolized by the masses.

Ends in many small lines Unsettled, with many conflicting interests.

Ends in a fork with prongs on Mounts of Mercury, Saturn and Apollo (6) Lasting success on a firm base.

TIMING EVENTS ON THE LINE OF THE SUN
The timeline for the line of the Sun is calculated in much the same way as the timeline for the line of fate (see page 164). A vertical line is drawn from the base of the Saturn (middle) finger to the first rascette of the wrist. The midpoint is taken to be 40 years (**a**). Five-, ten- and twenty- year intervals are then marked along this vertical line. The time gauge can then be transferred to the line of the Sun.

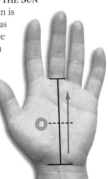

MARKS ON THE LINE OF THE SUN

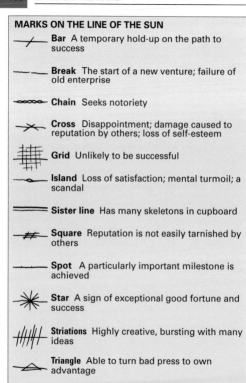

Bar A temporary hold-up on the path to success

Break The start of a new venture; failure of old enterprise

Chain Seeks notoriety

Cross Disappointment; damage caused to reputation by others; loss of self-esteem

Grid Unlikely to be successful

Island Loss of satisfaction; mental turmoil; a scandal

Sister line Has many skeletons in cupboard

Square Reputation is not easily tarnished by others

Spot A particularly important milestone is achieved

Star A sign of exceptional good fortune and success

Striations Highly creative, bursting with many ideas

Triangle Able to turn bad press to own advantage

GIRDLE OF VENUS

No line A well-controlled, calm personality, not one much concerned with the hidden meanings of life.

Well-marked Over-emotional, craves excitement and variety.

Short Keenly aware of the feelings of others.

Blurred or broken Over-sensitive.

Crosses lines of fate and line of the Sun (1) Witty and talented.

Ends on Mount of Mercury (2) Enormous reserves of energy, but a tendency to go to extremes as well as a tendency to introversion.

Runs off side of the hand instead of forming a semicircular shape (3) Vacillating, a ditherer.

VIA LASCIVA (MILKY WAY)

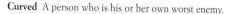

Straight Restless, easily bored. Can be a sign that the person has allergies, and for this reason the Via Lasciva is known also as the allergy line.

Straight and long, reaching mount of Mercury An eloquent speaker of dubious morality.

Curved A person who is his or her own worst enemy.

Curved, and beginning inside Mount of Venus (1) Liable to take things to excess. Someone who could easily become addicted – to drugs, alcohol, etc.

Branchline reaching to line of the Sun (2) Potential riches if the lines do not quite touch. Financial losses as the result of a relationship (e.g. an expensive divorce settlement) if they cross.

Runs off palm to wrist (3) Passionate, active and forceful.

RASCETTES (BRACELETS)

The top rascette is associated with health, the second rascette with wealth, and the third with love.

Parallel and clearly marked A healthy, wealthy, long and peaceful life.

Chainlike top bracelet (1) Eventual happiness after a difficult life.

Top bracelet arching into the palm in a woman's hand (2) Possible difficulties in childbirth.

Line from top bracelet to Mount of Jupiter A long and profitable journey.

Line from top bracelet to Mount of the Sun A trip to a hot country.

Top bracelet linked to Mount of Mercury Sudden riches.

Top bracelet linked to Mount of the Moon (3) Each line represents a journey.

HEPATICA (OR LINE OF HEALTH, OR LINE OF MERCURY)

No line A strong and healthy constitution, but this good health is perhaps taken for granted.

Deeply engraved Low physical resistance; tiredness. Can denote hypochondria.

Wavy (1) Digestive problems.

Blurred Lack of physical stamina.

Touches lifeline Take extra care of health at that time.

Begins on Mount of Venus (2) Works in health service or is particularly concerned with health issues.

Ends on lifeline (3) Constant nervous tension.

Blue patches Disorders of the brain.

MARKS ON HEPATICA

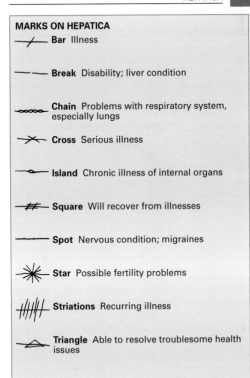

— Bar **Bar** Illness

— — **Break** Disability; liver condition

∞∞∞ **Chain** Problems with respiratory system, especially lungs

—✕— **Cross** Serious illness

—●— **Island** Chronic illness of internal organs

—#— **Square** Will recover from illnesses

——— **Spot** Nervous condition; migraines

✳ **Star** Possible fertility problems

////// **Striations** Recurring illness

△ **Triangle** Able to resolve troublesome health issues

LINE OF MARS (THE INNER LIFELINE)

If present Sustains life in time of illness or danger or represents a faithful lifelong companion.

LINES OF MARRIAGE

Strongly marked A marriage or close relationship. The number of lines indicates the number of such relationships.

Weakly marked Each line indicates a minor romantic attachment of little importance.

Long and straight A long and happy relationship.

Broken A divorce or separation.

Broken lines overlapping A reunion after a separation, perhaps remarriage to the same person.

Double line A relationship with two people at the same time, the relative depths of the relationships being indicated by the strength of the lines.

Curves downward Will outlive partner.

Curve upward to line of the Sun A marriage to a famous

or wealthy person if the lines do not quite touch. If the lines cross, the marriage will be unhappy.

Strong curve upward to base of little finger Staying unmarried but not celibate.

Starts with a fork Delay or frustration at the start of a relationship.

Ends in a fork A separation of some kind.

Crossed by a line running from base of finger of Mercury Opposition to a relationship.

Crossed by girdle of Venus An unhappy marriage, a nagging partner.

CHILD LINES

If present The lines run from the base of the finger of Mercury to the marriage lines. The number of lines are said to indicate the number of children, with the stronger lines representing boys, and the fainter lines girls.

TRAVEL LINES

If present Each line is thought to represent a journey to distant lands. Mars on the lines represents problematic journeys; clear lines reveal safe journeys.

LINE OF INTUITION

Semicircle beginning on Mount of Mercury and ending on Mount of the Moon An impressionable person who is sensitive to their surroundings. They are intuitive of others feelings, have strange warning dreams and some are even psychic.

MARKS ON THE LINE OF INTUITION

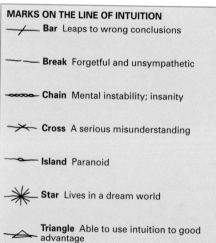

Bar Leaps to wrong conclusions

Break Forgetful and unsympathetic

Chain Mental instability; insanity

Cross A serious misunderstanding

Island Paranoid

Star Lives in a dream world

Triangle Able to use intuition to good advantage

RING LINES

1) Solomon's ring (or ring of Jupiter) If you have a line that forms a ring around the base of the index finger, then you are wise beyond your years.

2) Ring of Saturn This ring denotes the negative traits cynicism, melancholy and a depressive personality.

3) Ring of Apollo The presence of this ring indicates a lack of artistic appreciation or creative expression.

4) Family ring (or ring of Mercury) Denotes a strong sense of responsibility towards the family.

READING BETWEEN THE LINES

As well as analyzing the shape and position of lines on the hand, palmists also literally read between the lines. The area between the lines of head and heart should be a neat and well-defined oblong for the best possible portent of a balanced and steady progress through life – and nearly smooth, empty of all the collections of tiny lines found elsewhere. Otherwise there may be a tendency to imbalance, extremism of one kind or another and a somewhat erratic and fitful life. And the larger the triangular area formed by the lines of head, life and health, the better the omen.

COMPATIBILITY AND LINES ON THE PALM

There are so many factors to consider when analyzing the lines on the hand, that it is all but impossible to provide examples of every possible compatible variation.

HEADLINES AND COMPATIBILITY

In general, though, when comparing headlines, check the angle of curve. Two people who both have curved headlines (or two people who have straight headlines) are more likely to get on than a person with a straight headline and a person with a curved headline. This is because this trait reveals people's fundamental approach to life: those with straight headlines are practical and down-to-earth while those with curved headlines are take a broad, holistic view of life.

LIFELINES AND COMPATIBILITY

When comparing lifelines assess how they are formed. A person with a weakly formed, chained or faint lifeline that runs close to the mount of Venus is unlikely to get on with someone who has a strong, definite lifeline that curves wide around the mount of Venus. This is because the latter is bursting with energy while the former prefers a quiet life.

HEARTLINES AND COMPATIBILITY

Heartlines that indicate compatibility tend to follow similar paths across the palm and are of a similar length to each other; this shows that the two halves of the couple can understand each other's moods.

IDENTIFYING 'TYPES' OF LOVERS

It is possible to pick out the lines that would typically be
found on the hands of certain categories of lovers. It is not
necessary for every variation listed for each type of partner
to be present of the hand for that character analysis to
apply. Even one or two instances occurring, especially
when backed up by other signs on the hands, can reveal
the particular traits under discussion.

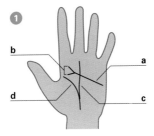

1 Steady partners

- low-lying heartline (**a**) indicates a down-to-earth, rational
  approach to love even though the person may well still be
  warm-hearted and generous
- a straight heartline (**a**) reveals that these people are
  unlikely to fall in love at first sight, they take time to
  decide if someone is right for them
- if the heartline ends in a fork (**b**) then your partner will
  be level-headed as well as romantic and affectionate
- if the fateline (**c**) starts at the lifeline (**d**), then the person
  has a strong sense of family responsibility

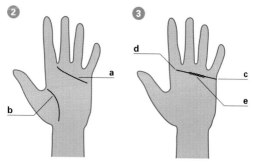

2 Shy lovers

- heartline ends between first and second fingers (**a**): caring people who do not wear their love on their sleeves even though they might love someone deeply. More likely to show their feelings through what they do
- lifelines that run close to or on edge of the Mount of Venus reveal a low sex drive (**b**)

3 Romantic, sensitive lovers

- a high-set straight heartline (**c**) indicates a spiritual lover, a romantic needs attention and support
- heartline ends on Mount of Jupiter (**d**): as well as signifying a romantic nature, this denotes a perfectionist attitude to romance, with high, perhaps unrealistic, expectations of the relationship and partner
- if your partner has a chained heartline (**e**) take extra care with their sensitive nature as they are easily hurt. (This can also be a sign of promiscuity.)

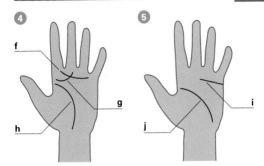

4 Passionate lovers

- girdle of Venus (**f**) is often present in passionate lovers
- a headline that sweeps upwards in a curve and ends under the Mount of Saturn (**g**) indicates passion and equals a strong sex drive as well as someone who likes to take the lead in bed. But people with steeply curved headlines can be vain about their partners, who they prefer to be good looking
- a strong lifeline (**h**) that sweeps well clear of the Mount of Venus indicates a strong sex drive

5 Bad signs

- short heartline (**i**): an irresponsible and unfaithful lover
- weak, chained or faint heartline: emotionally needy, insecure and likely to be taken advantage of
- islands on lifeline can indicate sexual problems
- lifeline that ends on Mount of the Moon (**j**) can indicate an inability to settle down

LINES AND HEALTH

There are so many different ways to assess health by reading the lines of the hand that careful study and great experience is needed really to be confident in such diagnoses. In general, though, clear strong lines indicate a more healthy person than weak or marked lines do, and there are certain signs that are typical of troublesome regions of the body. Consult the relevant pages on hepatica (see page 172) for further information on how to judge health by reading the lines on the hand.

SIGNS OF DELICATE CONSTITUTIONS OR POOR HEALTH
- broken or fragmented lifeline
- a series of fine striations on lifeline can denote a highly-strung nature
- many lines criss-crossing the palm can reveal stress or a nervous disposition
- islands on the lifeline can indicate lowered resistance to diseases
- generally, marks on lines are not good signs as they often indicate periods of illness, bad luck or low energy.

SIGNS OF A STRONG CONSTITUTION OR GOOD HEALTH
- long, strong lifeline
- line of Mars runs parallel to breaks in lifeline
- three strong unbroken rascettes
- clear, open hand without many secondary lines indicates a lack of stress and a balanced nervous system

SIGNS OF PARTICULAR PROBLEMS
- **A cross or star on palm** often refers to a sudden shock such as an accident or injury. On the heartline,

perhaps a heart problem, on headline it is likely to indicate a blow to the head, and on the lifeline it can reveal something leading to loss of consciousness: surgery or a coma, for example.

- **Clean break in fateline** reveals an accident or illness that affects employment.
- **Digestive problems (a)** are indicated by a patch of fine striations that cross plain of Mars at centre of palm.
- **Rheumatism (b)** revealed by a fine grid on the percussion.
- **Recurring headaches** are denoted by pin prick-like marks on the headline.
- **Allergies** are indicated by the Via Lasciva which appears as a horizontal line across Mount of the Moon (allergies)
- **Gynaecological problems** are pointed to when the top rascette arches onto palm and when a large diamond appears on the lifeline in middle third of lifeline.

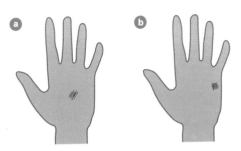

CAREERS IN THE LINES

Advertising or public relations executive
Curved headline • Line of intuition present • Curving heartline that rises on Mount of Jupiter

Accountant/Banker
Strong branch from heartline to Mount of Saturn • Straight and long headline • Clear and straight line of fate, if present • Heartline that cuts straight across the palm

Actor
Deep, curved heartline that begins on the Mount of Jupiter • Headline ends on Mount of the Moon • Line of the Sun marked with a star and ending on the Mount of Apollo

Artist
Headline sweeps towards Mount of the Moon • Strong line of the Sun • No ring of Apollo • Curved headline

Architect
Heartline with branches to Mounts of Jupiter and Saturn • straight headline • Line of intuition present but not vital

Athlete
Generally strong clear lines, especially lifeline • Inner lifeline present • Chained top rascette

Clairvoyant/Psychic
Line of intuition forms a perfect crescent • Headline dips into mount of the Moon

Clergyman/woman
Curving heartline rises on Mount of Jupiter, ending under Mount of Mercury • Forked headline • Line of intuition

present • Fragmented rascettes

Designer
Curved headline, often forked or reaching Mount of the Moon • Heartline rises on the Mount of Jupiter

Doctor
Medical stigmata present: short vertical lines on the Mount of Mercury • Hepatica begins on the Mount of Venus and crosses lifeline • Heartline long and curved • Headline cuts straight across palm

Entrepreneur
Head and lifeline distant • Strong hepatica • headline forks at the end nearest percussion • Strong, definite fateline • fateline that ends under first finger • Branch from fateline to the Mount of Mercury • Line of the Sun that sweeps out from lifeline • Star on the line of the Sun

Farmer or labourer
Short straight headline • Heartline that cuts straight across the palm • Strong, definite fateline • Headline slopes to reach top of Mount of Moon

Freelance worker
Fateline has several short parallel lines • Multiple lines of the Sun

Judge
Ring of Solomon present • Straight headline • Heartline linked to Mount of Jupiter

Lawyer
Ring of Solomon present • Straight headline • Clear and

deep lifeline, often with inner lifeline • Line of fate an advantage

Managing director
Striations (or stress lines) on fingertips • Palm criss-crossed with a dense network of secondary lines • Line of intuition present • Long, straight heartline

Media professional
Curved or forked headline, with branches to Mount of Moon and/or Upper mount of Mars • Heartline rises on Mount of Jupiter

Model
Numerous travel lines • Long line of the Sun • Fate line is fragmented

Musician
Strong line of the Sun

Nurse
Hepatica begins on the Mount of Venus and crosses lifeline • Medical stigmata present: short vertical lines on the Mount of Mercury • Ring of Solomon present • Heartline long and low

Politician
Fateline that ends under first finger • Line of the Sun present • Straight heartline rising on Mount of Jupiter

Poet
Headline sweeps towards Mount of the Moon • Line of intuition forms a perfect crescent • Complete girdle of Venus present • No ring of Apollo

Salesperson
Heartline rising on the Mount of Jupiter or Saturn and ending on Mount of Mercury • Straight headline linked to Mount of Jupiter

Stand-up comedian
Lifeline swings out in a wide semicircle towards the centre of the palm

Scientist/Technology expert
Strong, clear, straight headline tied to lifeline • Heartline rises between mounts of Jupiter and Saturn • Strong lifeline • Branches link heart and head lines

Teacher
Heartline rising on Mount of Jupiter or with a branch to this mount • Ring of Solomon present • Long headline that is straight (in the case of science teachers) or dips to Mount of Moon (in the case of arts teachers)

Tour guide (or other regular traveller)
Lifeline sweeps towards percussion • Branch from lifeline sweeps over to Mount of the Moon • Strong line of the Sun • Numerous travel lines

Writer
Headline sweeps towards Mount of the Moon • Fork appears in the headline beneath the Mount of Apollo • No ring of Apollo • Strong headline, more so than the heartline • Girdle of Venus is present • Heartline rises on mount of Jupiter and has many fine branches • Many minor lines present

Glossary

Apollo In the ancient Greek and Roman pantheons, Apollo was the god of sun and youth. In palmistry, the ring finger and the mount at its base are named after Apollo.

Aquarius The Western Zodiac sign for those born between 20 January and 18 February. The basal (bottom) phalange of the Mercury finger is associated with this sign.

Aries The Western Zodiac sign for those born between 21 March and 19 April. The initial (top) phalange of the Apollo finger is associated with this sign.

Cancer The Western Zodiac sign for those born between 21 June and 22 July. The initial (top) phalange of the Jupiter finger is associated with this sign.

Capricorn The Western Zodiac sign for those born between 22 December and 19 January. The initial (top) phalange of the Saturn finger is associated with this sign.

cheiro (or chiro) The ancient Greek word for *hand*.

cheirognomy Discerning character by the shape and form of the hands. Cheirognomists study the shape of the hand and the length and set of fingers in particular.

cheirology Analyzing hands to reveal character.

cheiromancy Foretelling the future by reading the hand.

cheiromant Someone who practises cheiromancy.

cheiropracter A palmist.

cheirosophy The ancient Greek term for the study of hand symbology and hand analysis.

cheirotype The classification of a hand according to its cheirognomic features.

chirognomy See cheirognomy.

chirology See cheirology.

chiromancy See cheiromancy.

chiromant See cheiromant.

chiropracter See cheiropracter.

chirosophy See cheirosophy.

conic A hand or finger shape recognizable for being wider at base than top, giving the feature a tapered shape.

dermatoglyphics The study of skin ridge patterns.

Gemini The Western Zodiac sign for those born between 21 May and 20 June. The middle phalange of the Mercury finger is associated with this sign.

index finger The first (or Jupiter) finger.

Jupiter In the ancient Roman pantheon, Jupiter was the king of the gods; he was named after the ancient Greek god, Zeus. In palmistry, the index finger and the mount at its base are named after Jupiter

Jupiter finger The index finger.

Leo The Western Zodiac sign for those born between 23 July and 22 August. The basal phalange of the Apollo finger is associated with this sign.

Libra The Western Zodiac sign for those born between 23 September and 22 October. The initial (top) phalange of the Mercury finger is associated with this sign.

Mars In the ancient Roman pantheon, Mars was the god of war; he was named after the ancient Greek god, Aries. In palmistry, two mounts on the palm are named after Mars.

Mercury In the ancient Roman pantheon, Mercury was t he messenger of the gods; he was named after the ancient Greek god, Hermes. In palmistry, the little finger and the mount at its base are named after Mercury.

Mercury finger The little finger.

middle finger Also known as the Saturn finger.

Moon In palmistry, the semicircle sometimes visible at base of a fingernail.

mount A fleshy pad on the palm of hand.

palmar Of, or on, the palm.

palmar quadrants The four divisions of the palm.

palmist Someone who practises palmistry.

palmistry The study of the hand to reveal character and, more traditionally, to foretell the future.

percussion The outside edge of the palm.

phalanges Those parts of the fingers between the joints.

Pisces The Western Zodiac sign for those born between 19 February and 20 March. The middle phalange of the Jupiter finger is associated with this sign.

rascettes The 'bracelets' formed by wrinkles on wrist.

ring finger The finger next to the little finger; also known as the Apollo finger.

Sagitarrius The Western Zodiac sign for those born between 22 November and 21 December. The middle phalange of the Apollo finger is associated with this sign.

Saturn In the ancient Roman pantheon, Saturn was the god of time; he was named after the ancient Greek god, Kronos. In palmistry, the middle finger and the mount at its base are named after Saturn.

Saturn finger The middle finger.

Scorpio The Western Zodiac sign for those born between 23 October and 21 November. The basal (bottom) phalange of the Jupiter finger is associated with this sign.

spatulate Literally means spade-like, and is used in palmistry to describe the shape of fingers and hands.

striations A series of vertical lines.

Sun finger Another name for the ring, or Apollo, finger.

Taurus The Western Zodiac sign for those born between 20 April and 20 May. The basal (bottom) phalange of the Saturn finger is associated with this sign.

tri radius A triangular fingerprint ridge pattern that allows identification of fingerprint type.

Venus In the ancient Roman pantheon, Venus was the goddess of love; she was named after the ancient Greek goddess, Aphrodite. In palmistry, the large mount at the base of the thumb is named after Venus.

Virgo The Western Zodiac sign for those born between 23 August and 22 September. The middle phalange of the Saturn finger is associated with this sign.

Index